"Healing from dysfunctional relationship patterns can be enormously challenging. In *The Toxic Relationship Recovery Workbook*, Krystal gently leads readers through the process of meaningful change by helping them explore their relationship dynamics and attachment styles. Using clinical examples and awareness-building questions, this book offers readers research-informed information, emotional validation, and practical skills aimed at healing the past while confidently developing healthier relationships moving forward."

—**Cortney S. Warren, PhD, ABPP**, board-certified clinical psychologist, and author of *Letting Go of Your Ex*

"I love a good workbook—and *The Toxic Relationship Recovery Workbook* delivers! As a therapist, I find the attachment-based framework invaluable for helping clients understand their patterns and build secure relationships. This practical, supportive workbook is ideal for those leaving unhealthy relationships and ready to heal."

—**Sharon Martin, DSW, LCSW**, psychotherapist, and author of *Cutting Ties with Your Parents* and *The Better Boundaries Workbook*

THE TOXIC RELATIONSHIP RECOVERY WORKBOOK

Understand and Heal Attachment Wounds,
Reclaim Your Confidence, and
Build the Healthy Relationships You Deserve

KRYSTAL MAZZOLA WOOD, LMFT

New Harbinger Publications, Inc.

Publisher's Note

New Harbinger Publications is an employee-owned company.

New Harbinger Publications, Inc.
5720 Shattuck Avenue
Oakland, CA 94609
www.newharbinger.com

Cover design by Amy Shoup

Acquired by Ryan Buresh

Edited by Rebecca Job

Library of Congress Cataloging-in-Publication Data on file

Printed in the United States of America

28 27 26

10 9 8 7 6 5 4 3 2 1 First Printing

To my younger self—Krystal, thank you for holding on to hope even in your darkest moments. You were right to hold on and you made it to the other side. Your life is more loving, safe, and beautiful than you ever even imagined. I truly couldn't be here without you. I love you unconditionally.

CONTENTS

Chapter 1

STARTING YOUR RECOVERY JOURNEY

Welcome to this next step in your personal evolution! You are exhibiting tremendous internal strength and courage being here with this workbook. Arriving at this moment likely has not been an easy or smooth journey. Before getting here, perhaps you thought about leaving your toxic relationship for years. Maybe it seems like this is the eighty-third time you've tried to walk away, and you feel skeptical if you can really stay away this time. Or you may have picked up this workbook hoping it'll help you find the courage to finally leave.

Wherever you find yourself, and whatever your emotions, know you're in the right place. There is no shame in having found yourself in a toxic relationship. There are valid and understandable reasons for this, which will be discussed in later chapters. However, for now, please know there is no need to get stuck in embarrassment or self-judgment. Truly, the most important thing is you are here now, and you are not alone.

All people sometimes find themselves in places of suffering they wouldn't wish even on their worst enemy. And yet, healing is always possible—and it all starts with one act of courage, such as picking up this workbook. I know this intimately, as I've been on both sides of this journey. The steps in this workbook are influenced by both my professional and my personal experience. As a licensed marriage and family therapist, I've supported countless clients in recovering from toxic relationship patterns and healing their attachment style. Furthermore, in my own life, I applied the concepts you will learn here to personally recover from an anxious-avoidant attachment style and almost two decades of being trapped in toxic relationship cycles. With consistent practice and baby steps, you truly can transform your entire life. I'm so grateful that there is at least a part of you that feels hopeful to connect to this truth. Thank you from the bottom of my heart for being here on this journey with me.

How to Use This Book

This workbook is your guide as you recover. Each chapter builds off previous ones to move you from any pain, confusion, or stuckness you may feel to greater clarity and security. To experience this relief, you will focus on your own healing. To truly break out of toxic relationship patterns, you must focus on yourself. Even if you hope to heal your toxic relationship, it's simply ineffective to focus on anyone else's change process rather than your own.

This workbook is written as if you have recently left your toxic relationship. However, if you are still in a toxic relationship, this workbook is also for you. It's completely understandable if you don't feel you want to leave or don't feel ready to do so. Please just adjust any words such as "ex" to "partner" to fit your situation.

The exercises in this workbook come from attachment-based therapy to help you become more securely attached. When you are securely attached, your relationships change. You believe in your worth and you *know* that you are completely capable of attracting—and maintaining—a relationship with a person you feel truly safe, connected, and intimate with. You will learn more about attachment theory in a later chapter.

As you commit to your healing with this workbook, you may find yourself feeling even more insecurity, anxiety, or confusion. If so, please know this means you are on the right path! When things are improving, the middle of the change typically looks the messiest. Just like when you're reorganizing a closet, it's right in the middle of this change that your space looks most chaotic! If you feel a little worse at times, know you are truly in the midst of powerful transformation. Please keep going to experience the relief, empowerment, and clarity on the other side of this temporary disruption.

As you recover, it is naturally painful sometimes to remember details of your toxic relationship. You may feel grief as well as shame, recalling how you may have allowed your ex to treat you because you didn't believe you were worth more or capable of having options. It may also be painful to remember how you may have hurt or pushed away your ex at times out of your own insecurities or fear of intimacy. In fact, writing this workbook brought up old painful feelings of my own that needed processing. To truly recover—and stay in recovery—we must be willing to acknowledge, feel, and process these old feelings even if they hurt. Processing these old emotions allows us to move forward with positive intention rather than old reactivity. Finally, intense emotions are not a sign of "failure" or a lack of recovery. They only mean you are human.

This workbook can be used on your own, with a trusted friend, or with the support of a licensed therapist. You don't need to do this alone. In fact, part of being a securely attached person is seeking support when needed. For help finding support, please refer to the Resources section. To give you extra support, case studies are provided throughout this workbook as well. These examples are to help you connect with the activity further and brainstorm how it personally relates to you. Finally, there is also an array of free online tools available to further enhance your experience with the workbook, which you can access at http://www.newharbinger.com/55992.

Overview of the Recovery Process

This workbook is your road map toward recovery. Of course, healing isn't linear, but this road map is created from tried-and-true techniques that, when applied together, simplify the process. Recovering from a toxic relationship pattern involves five primary steps, which are:

1. **Being Honest with Yourself**—You are honest about your past, thoughts, and feelings. This involves being honest about the truth of your ex and yourself. This self-awareness builds clarity and reduces self-doubt.

2. **Giving Yourself Grace and Understanding**—Often, toxic relationships degrade self-esteem, which manifests, in part, as harsh thoughts toward yourself. While understandable, this self-criticism often feeds the shame that keeps us stuck in toxic patterns.

3. **Soothing Your Emotions**—Being in a toxic relationship often feels like being on an emotional roller coaster—and recovery sometimes does too. Learning how to soothe your emotions kindly and effectively is an essential step in the recovery process.

4. **Caring for Yourself**—Do you notice that you put yourself last on your to-do list? Maybe this happened by caring for your ex, working too much, or just not doing the things you know would make you feel better. While completely common, healing requires showing up for yourself consistently.

5. **Living in the Present for a Healthier Future**—Throughout this healing process, there may be times you feel you just can't get "over" your past. This is understandable yet, unfortunately, no matter how poorly your ex (or anyone else) may have treated you, you cannot actually go back in time. Therefore, to truly recover, you must learn to live in the present. This then helps you create a future that's healthier.

You don't need to know how to practice all these steps yet. This is why you're here! At this point, just notice that there is a road map for your recovery process, *and* you will be supported along the way there.

• CASE STUDY: *Tylah and Nate*

Tylah met Nate in high school. After growing up in a loud, chaotic home, Tylah found Nate's quiet nature a welcome relief. She quickly fell in love and had a child with him at the end of high school. Once their son Tyson was born, Nate became detached, expecting Tylah to do all the childcare and housework because he had a job. When she would get tired or overwhelmed, he would give her the silent treatment. If she asked for connection, he'd tell her that he no longer found her attractive after the baby. She discovered he was cheating on her with a coworker five months ago. She just got the courage to leave and temporarily moved in with her sister.

EXERCISE: Being Honest with Yourself

Inner conflict, self-doubt, and judgments of yourself and the other person, including harshly blaming them, are common experiences in a toxic relationship. Often, people in toxic relationships talk themselves out of what they *know* deep down, such as by minimizing abuse that's going on or denying a partner is lying. Often, minimizing reality goes a step further by also questioning yourself. Here, you may have thought you're "too hard" on your ex or you were "expecting too much." You may have also experienced inner conflict, such as a part wanting to leave and a part wanting to cling to your ex. Or you may have obscured the truth that some of your own behaviors may have contributed to your ex acting in ways you thought were "crazy." Deep down though, you may feel conflicted, as you know that blaming them alone isn't the complete truth. To recover, it's important to be honest with yourself about your feelings, thoughts, behaviors, and conflicting desires. It's also important to be honest about your ex despite your hopes, inner conflict, and the potential you may see in them. When you're honest with yourself, you reduce the inner conflict that perpetuates toxic relationship cycles.

Please fill in the following prompts:

I first knew things were wrong in my relationship when:

____

____

____

____

At that time, my intuition or gut told me:

____

____

____

The choice I made at that point was:

____

____

____

I made this choice because:

____

____

____

How much time did I spend denying things felt wrong, and what actions did I take to distract myself?

____

____

____

The impact of the ways I distracted myself—and this investment of time—on my mental, physical, and financial health is:

____

____

____

If I expressed my doubts to my ex about them or the relationship, my ex would tell me:

____

____

____

What I thought or felt about this was:

____

____

____

How long did I try to make this relationship work?

____

____

____

What strategies did I try to make this relationship work?

____

____

____

____

How I felt about myself in this relationship was:

____

____

What did my loved ones say about this relationship or about how my ex treated me (and/or did I hide what was really happening from them)?

____

____

____

____

____

What was the final straw that made me leave the relationship (or pick up this workbook)?

____

____

____

____

After completing this exercise, thoughts of self-judgment may arise. These thoughts may be even more intense if you are still in this relationship. Please just notice these thoughts right now, as your self-talk may reflect what you allow others to say to you and what you think you're worth.

Example as Tylah

I knew things were wrong as soon as I had Tyson. Nate completely stopped engaging with me and wanted nothing to do with us. My gut told me that he was not going to be a good partner or father. I chose to ignore this because I didn't want my son to grow up without his dad like I did. I tried to be the perfect mom and housewife to ignore what I felt deep down. I blamed myself for Nate's lack of interest and thought if I could get my body back and never complain, we'd be a happy family. I only ended up feeling worse and more burned-out when Nate continued to be cold despite how hard I was working. When I did express my overwhelm, Nate would tell me to suck it up because he didn't like his job either. I thought I was being too hard on him, and I've tried for three years to ignore things. All my efforts to be "better" and not complain never changed things. I feel like my self-esteem is zero now. When I told my sister a few months ago about things, and how he cheated, she said that I deserve better. She also said that having no dad is better than watching his dad mistreat his mom. The final straw was overhearing Nate making plans to hook up later with his coworker. I can't live like this.

EXERCISE: Being Understanding with Yourself

You may often be self-critical. Perhaps your toxic partner was unkind, and you now repeat their words to yourself as an inner soundtrack. Or maybe these critical thoughts emerged much younger in life, perhaps due to a critical parent. This inner critic may also have originated from living in a culture that equates your worth with your productivity. Whatever the case, to break out of this negative self-talk cycle, which keeps you in toxic patterns, it's important to be kinder to yourself. This process involves self-validation. Validation is when you say why someone's thoughts, feelings, needs, and actions *make sense* given what you know about them. Self-validation is the practice of giving yourself this understanding.

You will begin to practice self-validation with the following prompts:

Describe any automatic judgmental thoughts you experienced during the previous exercise.

Example: I can't believe I'm in this situation—what's wrong with me?

____

____

____

____

Now describe any thoughts of self-doubt that may be creeping in.

Example: I'm a horrible mother for not making it work with my son's dad. If only I had been prettier and happier, none of this would have happened.

Now, consider how you'd approach a friend who has these same thoughts. You'd probably never be so harsh toward them but would comfort them instead. Can you do this for yourself by expressing understanding for your past decisions?

Example: I stayed because I wanted to be loved, and I wanted my son to have his dad. Also, I wanted to get back to the real him I met that was so kind.

If you are still in your toxic relationship, or want your ex back, what are the reasons for this?

Example: Of course, I sometimes want to get back with Nate. He's not a bad person and I love him. Plus, he's my son's dad.

If you feel self-doubt or inner conflict, can you remind yourself of all the effort you've already put into this relationship, and what the outcome was?

Example: I tried for three years to make Nate happy. All that happened is I feel I lost myself, lost precious time with my son, and I feel more self-hatred.

Now you'll take this practice of self-kindness a step further by truly comforting yourself. Place your hand over your heart space and take a breath. Repeat these understanding things to yourself aloud. It's okay if it feels uncomfortable or cheesy. Healing requires doing new, wiser things that may be unfamiliar or strange to you at first.

Example: [With hand on heart space] "It makes sense I overlooked how cold Nate was to me and tried to ignore his cheating at first. I really wanted to be loved, and this was the closest thing to love I had experienced."

Great job!

EXERCISE: Being Honest about Your Emotions

Another important part of being kinder to yourself involves caring for your emotions. Initially this may be challenging, because to survive your toxic relationship you may have developed a pattern of ignoring or numbing your emotions. Therefore, to effectively soothe your emotions, you must first become aware of them.

Currently, you likely have many complicated emotions. Some of these you may be very aware of while others may be less conscious. Whatever you feel, please know intense emotions are a natural part of having experienced a toxic relationship. There are no bad or wrong emotions to feel. It's also absolutely okay if they seem contradictory, such as resentment toward your ex and desire for them.

For this exercise, please identify any and all emotions you are aware of right now. Know this is just a snapshot in time and emotions naturally move and evolve. You don't need to figure out how to cope with them just yet. And if you find yourself judging them, try to validate why it *makes sense* you may feel this way, as you practiced before.

Please circle any and all emotions you notice feeling right now:

Anger	Resentment	Guilt	Self-doubt
Insecurity	Jealousy	Embarrassment	Confusion
Depression	Anxiety	Hopelessness	Love
Happiness	Gratitude	Relief	Despair
Nervousness	Urge to control	Self-loathing	Uncertainty

Longing (missing partner and/or life together or pets)

Add any emotions you can think of that aren't listed here:

____

____

____

EXERCISE: Affirming Your Emotions

Once you acknowledge an emotion, you have many options for coping well with it. One helpful option is to notice you don't have to get stuck in judging your emotions. Nor do you have to automatically react to them. Just because you feel something doesn't mean you have to act on it. For instance, just because you miss your ex doesn't mean you have to text them.

In this exercise, you will practice simply allowing and affirming an emotion's right to exist.

1. Look at the emotions you circled in the previous exercise. It's okay if you think any of these emotions are "bad" or confusing. At the same time, you have the right to feel them, and they do actually make sense.

2. Now fill in the following sentence for all the emotions you felt above and repeat the affirmation aloud

   "I feel ________________________ [insert emotion]. And I have the right to feel ________________________ [insert emotion]. It's a natural human emotion and others would feel this way too in the same scenario."

3. Repeat for all your current emotions.

4. Note your reactions to this exercise here:

   ____

   ____

   ____

   ____

   ____

   ____

   ____

EXERCISE: Protecting Your Well-Being by Letting Go

Part of self-care is letting go of what doesn't serve you, which includes your patterns, thoughts, and the way you treat yourself. In this exercise, you will consider the triggers that make you feel worse about your toxic relationship. Then you will practice setting a boundary around one, or more, of these triggers. This act of self-protection builds self-respect, which may have been depleted in your relationship.

1. Consider what current triggers you have that make you feel worse about your ex or being in your toxic relationship. Circle these triggers in the list below:

   - Seeing them on social media
   - My phone (including because I want to text/call them or continue to check to see if they've reached out)
   - Photos

- Gifts they gave me that are in my home
- Items they left at my place
- Certain types of music
- Seeing damage they caused to my property (e.g., a hole in the wall)
- Hanging out with mutual friends
- Certain bars/restaurants
- Write in anything else you can think of that triggers you to feel worse about the relationship:

  ____

  ____

  ____

  ____

  ____

2. Now consider what triggers you are ready to let go of to protect your well-being. Circle any you feel ready to release. (Note: If you're still in the relationship, you can still let go of triggers that make you feel worse or more conflicted to help create space for clarity and peace.)

- Donating an item (or more than one) that makes me think of them
- Not listening to music that triggers me
- Unfollowing them on social media
- Repairing damage they caused to my property or throwing the damaged item away
- Not going to certain places for now even if I like them because it makes me feel bad
- Asking mutual friends to not update me about my ex
- Deleting my social media
- Blocking their number
- Leaving my phone in another room to reduce the temptation to keep checking it (or fighting with them via text)

- Deleting photos
- Deleting text messages

If you feel stuck and are not ready to let go of much—or anything today—please know that just contemplating letting go is an important step of recovery.

3. Take a moment to let go of this item if possible or schedule a time for later. Consider the things you'd like to let go of (even if you're not ready) and how to do so, such as deleting them off social media. What are you considering that would be helpful to let go of? Write that here:

____

____

____

____

____

Now list the pros/cons of holding on vs. letting go.

Holding On

Pros	Cons

Letting Go

Pros	Cons

You are doing amazing work! Know you're already practicing the various steps of toxic relationship recovery! You are practicing kind self-awareness, while also letting go of what doesn't serve you. This helps you become more present rather than potentially obsessing about your toxic past. When you are more mindful and present, you can create the future you really want, rather than simply reacting to the past.

EXERCISE: Building Hope for the Future

Sticking with the recovery process is not always easy. While it's worth it, it's not without its challenges. As you go through this workbook, you may naturally question your efforts to recover at times. To help your future self who may feel discouraged, you will lean into your hope right now. After all, you wouldn't be here right now without hope. In those challenging moments, this hope is your greatest asset.

For this activity, you will consider what your life is like now—and imagine what it will be like once you have recovered. To start, please fill in each aspect of the following pie chart with a drawing or a few words that describe where you are currently. Please let yourself draw and be creative without self-censoring or judgment. This is part of giving yourself grace; remember, it's for your eyes only (stick figures are absolutely okay!). As a reminder, you may feel conflicting emotions in these categories (e.g., both needy toward your ex and resentful).

MY LIFE NOW

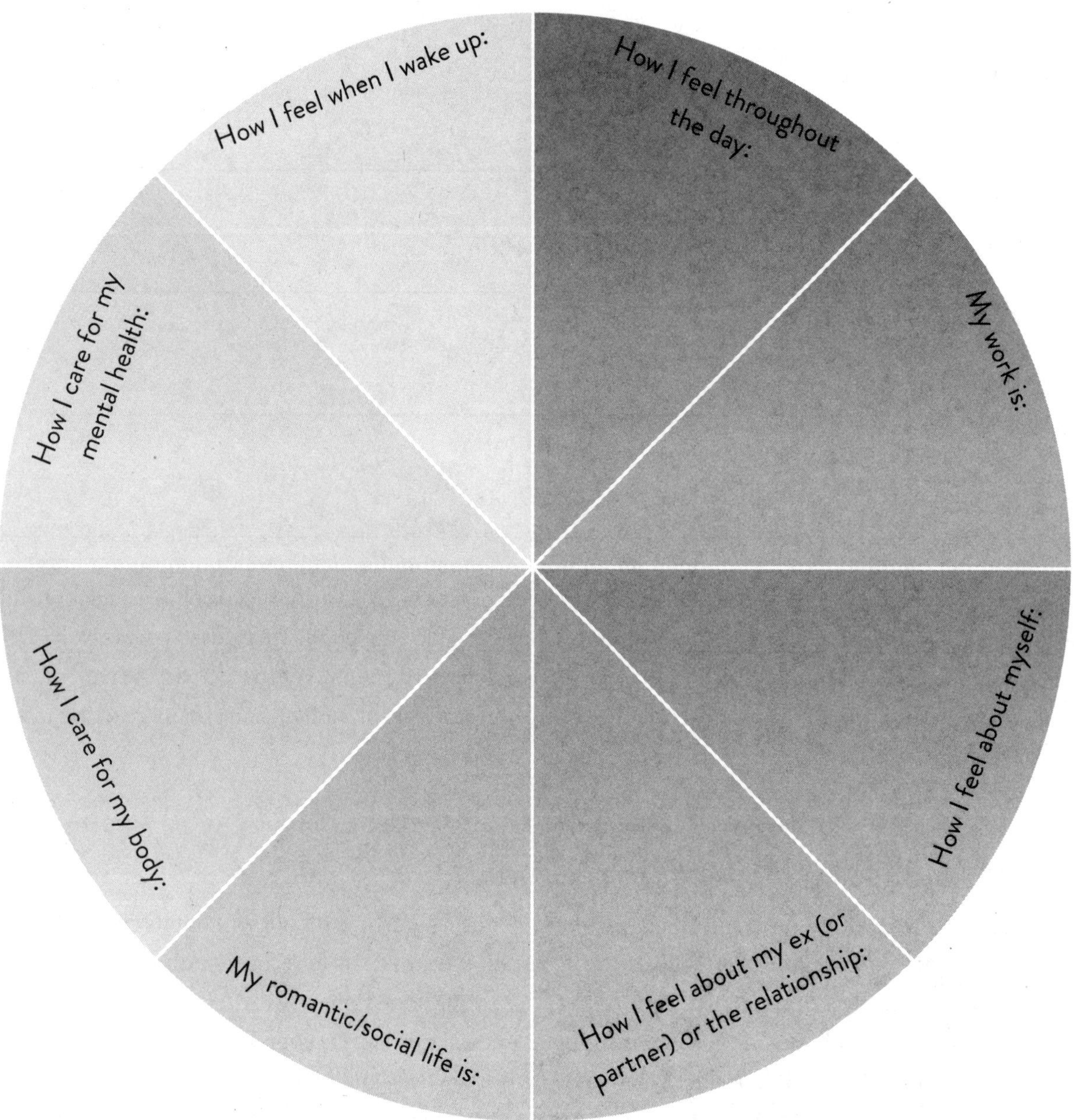

Wherever you find yourself today, that's okay. The most important thing is you are here now. Now take a moment to think about *why* you are completing this workbook. Consider the future you are hopeful to have once you recover. This hope is one of your most important allies to keep you committed to the recovery process.

Please complete this next pie chart *with the end in mind* as if you have already recovered. Once you have recovered, how will these aspects of your life have changed? Consider the changes you'd love to experience. Recovery truly has the power to transform your whole life.

MY LIFE IN THE FUTURE

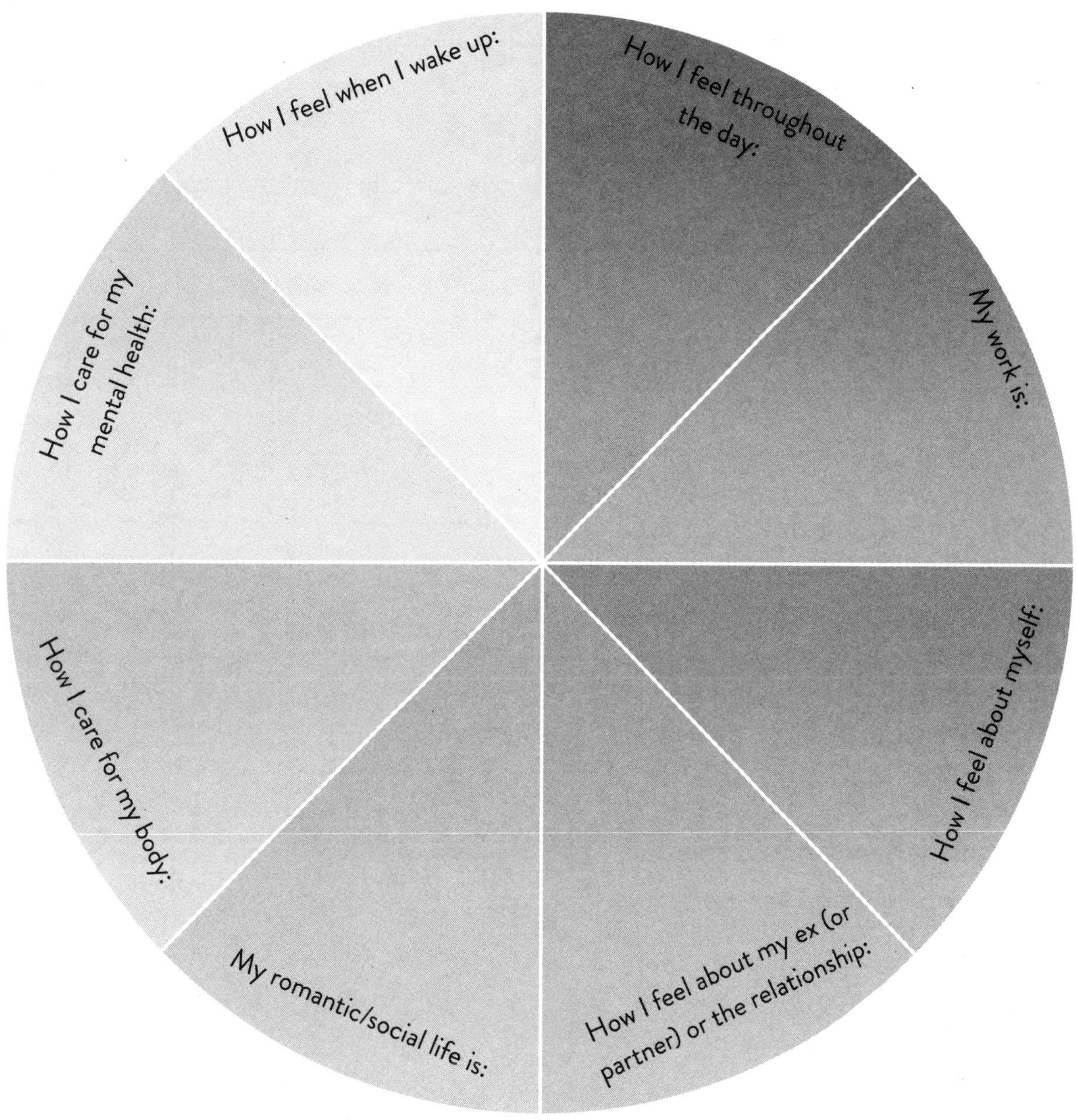

What thoughts or feelings arise as you notice the seeds you are planting for your future here? Your future is truly based on the hope you nurture throughout this process.

TYLAH NOW

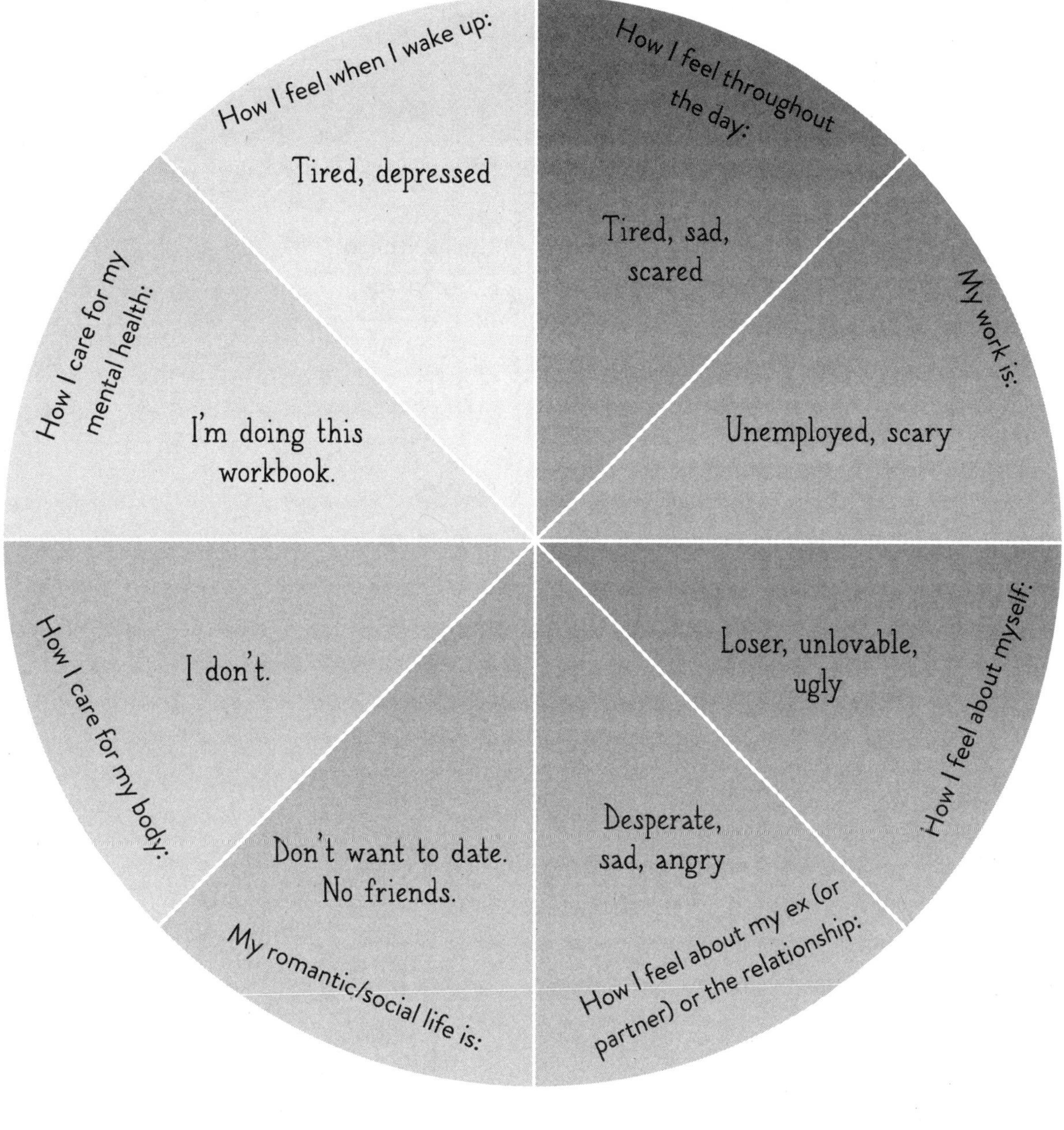
How I feel when I wake up:
Tired, depressed
How I feel throughout the day:
Tired, sad, scared
My work is:
Unemployed, scary
How I feel about myself:
Loser, unlovable, ugly
How I feel about my ex (or partner) or the relationship:
Desperate, sad, angry
My romantic/social life is:
Don't want to date. No friends.
How I care for my body:
I don't.
How I care for my mental health:
I'm doing this workbook.

TYLAH IN THE FUTURE

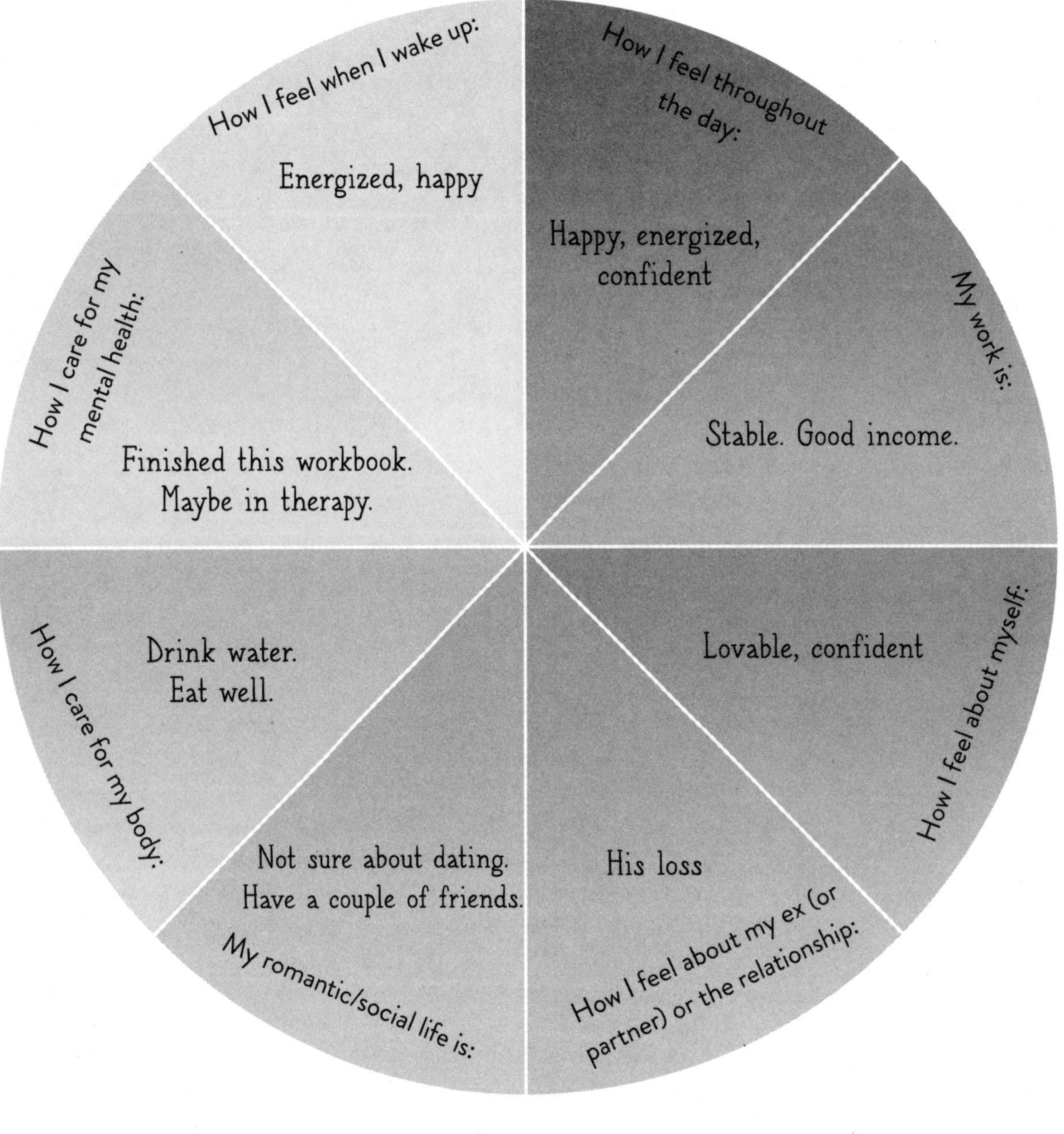

Starting Your Recovery Journey
Chapter Reminders

- Feeling a mix of emotions is completely natural. You may have a part that dislikes your ex *and* another that wants them back. Or you may feel hopeful *and* also cynical about your ability to recover sometimes.

- Internal conflict is a part of being human (and something we'll address more later).

- Healing isn't linear. Sometimes, it feels like you take two steps forward and then one back. Other times, you may feel "stuck."

- When you're truly recovering, it often feels like things feel worse before they get better. If this happens, know it's proof you're exactly on track—and please keep going!

- Honesty and kindness toward yourself will be some of your greatest resources on this journey.

- Your hopeful part only needs to be 1 percent bigger than your skeptical part for you to recover. Sticking with this process guarantees your recovery. If you ever feel discouraged, come back to your future-self pie chart.

- Finally—the work you are doing will be emotional or challenging at times, but you and your life are worth it! The work you do now will pay you back more than you can imagine over the rest of your life!

Chapter 2

TOXIC RELATIONSHIPS 101

You're here because you *know* you've been in a toxic relationship. And yet, sometimes, the exact definition of a toxic relationship can feel a little unclear. To help your recovery process, it's important to define what exactly makes a relationship toxic.

A toxic relationship is a relationship that is extremely harmful or poisonous to the well-being of one, or both, partners. Well-being includes your mental, physical, social, sexual, emotional, spiritual, and financial health.

Based on this definition, we can see that, among other things, a toxic relationship can:

- Erode your self-esteem
- Fill you with anxiety
- Estrange you from friends and family
- Stress you out and cause a sense of burnout
- Make your thinking foggy
- Contribute to obsessive thinking
- Leave you feeling depressed or hopeless
- Make you feel disconnected from others or lonely
- Hurt your physical health by depleting your immune system, leaving you chronically ill, filled with muscle aches, or experiencing high blood pressure or heart issues due to chronic stress (American Heart Association 2024)
- Drain your energy, leaving you exhausted all the time no matter how much you sleep
- Degrade you sexually and/or make you sexually insecure
- Lead to financial instability, debt, or bankruptcy

As you read this list and definition, you may notice how your own well-being was harmed in your relationship. You may also notice how your partner was impacted too.

Toxic Relationships Are Dysfunctional

A relationship in its healthy state of functioning is safe and loving. On the other hand, toxic relationships are dysfunctional. This term may sound strange or clinical, yet it simply means that the relationship isn't working well. To clarify the differences you may anticipate in a securely attached partnership, it's helpful to highlight dysfunctional relationship qualities (Gottman 2011). Please read through this list of toxic relationship qualities while highlighting and adding notes to the ones you personally experienced:

- More stress and conflict than peace and harmony
- Fights that go from 0 to 100 where one or both partners are defensive and critical
- The silent treatment
- Never actually resolving fights but just brushing things under the rug
- Ignoring each other—or worse, becoming angry when your partner wants attention
- Seeing the worst in each other (even making up bad things others don't see)
- Constantly feeling like you're walking on eggshells
- In heterosexual relationships, the man second-guessing the woman's thoughts, opinions, needs, and boundaries. For example, he may say, "Who told you that?" when she shares something insightful rather than trusting her intellect.

Toxic vs. Abusive

The qualities of a toxic relationship naturally make them harmful to your well-being in one or more ways. When abuse is present, this harm is further intensified. Abuse may be psychological, emotional, spiritual, financial, sexual, and/or physical in nature. Physical abuse tends to be the most obvious. This includes hitting, slapping, pushing, choking, and kicking. Other forms of abuse may be, at times, less clear. For example, it's very common that when people experience psychological abuse, they second-guess themselves and wonder whether they're "too sensitive."

Psychological abuse includes mental, verbal, and emotional attacks. Common examples of such abuse include contempt, name-calling, and gaslighting. Contempt is when one partner acts superior to the other. This includes harsh sarcasm and mocking the other person even when they pass it off as a joke. A person who is psychologically abusive demeans their partner's thoughts, emotions, and entire self. Being controlled or monitored is also highly abusive. Financial abuse is another serious and common problem in abusive relationships. This includes being prevented from seeking employment and all your access to money being withheld.

An abusive relationship can cause significant trauma. At times, a person may develop post-traumatic stress disorder (PTSD). This includes having nightmares or intrusive flashbacks related to the abuse. You may feel constantly "on guard," startle easily, or feel disconnected from your body. If you believe your toxic, abusive relationship may have caused you trauma, it is recommended you work with a trauma therapist. This workbook will support you in healing aspects of your wounding. But healing the trauma and the lasting impacts of an abusive relationship—or helping you plan on how to safely exit an abusive relationship—is outside the scope of this workbook. Please work with a qualified trauma therapist with experience treating domestic violence. The Resources section will help you find one in your area.

EXERCISE: Assess How Toxic Your Relationship Was for Your Well-Being

Here you will assess how damaging your relationship was to your well-being. Often in toxic relationships, people are confused about what's really happening. To support your recovery, it's important to gain clarity. Furthermore, an essential first step of healing is you must "name it to tame it," as psychiatrist Dan Siegel says (Siegel and Bryson 2012). These questions will have you consider not only your past partner's behaviors but your own behaviors as well. This may feel challenging, yet to fully recover from toxic patterns it's important to consider both sides. Please take your time and take breaks from this exercise as needed. You do not have to force healing—it always happens in its own due time.

Please rate how true or untrue each statement is regarding your toxic relationship:

1. I hid the truth about my relationship from friends and family because I was scared of them judging my partner and/or wanting me to leave. Alternatively, I hid how I treated my partner to not be judged poorly.

   Never ❖ Rarely ❖ Sometimes ❖ Often ❖ Always

2. I did things that could jeopardize my health, such as binge drinking or eating, having unprotected sex with someone I don't know, or self-harming (for example, slapping or cutting myself) when I was upset about my relationship.

   Never ❖ Rarely ❖ Sometimes ❖ Often ❖ Always

3. We could not discuss the things we disagreed about without being defensive or bringing up other problems.

   Never ❖ Rarely ❖ Sometimes ❖ Often ❖ Always

4. We swept things under the rug just to get along again.

   Never ❖ Rarely ❖ Sometimes ❖ Often ❖ Always

5. My partner's words and actions didn't match up a lot of the time. And/or I had a pattern of lying.

Never ❖ Rarely ❖ Sometimes ❖ Often ❖ Always

6. Fights seemed to go from 0 to 100.

Never ❖ Rarely ❖ Sometimes ❖ Often ❖ Always

7. I made excuses for my partner. Or my partner made a lot of excuses for me.

Never ❖ Rarely ❖ Sometimes ❖ Often ❖ Always

8. I felt like I was walking on eggshells with my partner.

Never ❖ Rarely ❖ Sometimes ❖ Often ❖ Always

9. When we argued, we could not find the middle ground or compromise.

Never ❖ Rarely ❖ Sometimes ❖ Often ❖ Always

10. My partner would tell me that I don't really think or feel the way I do—or would argue why the way I think or feel is wrong. And/or vice versa.

Never ❖ Rarely ❖ Sometimes ❖ Often ❖ Always

11. My partner blamed me for all the problems in the relationship. They would never apologize. Or I never took accountability for any issues.

Never ❖ Rarely ❖ Sometimes ❖ Often ❖ Always

12. We have broken up only to get back together at least once.

Never ❖ Rarely ❖ Sometimes ❖ Often ❖ Always

13. I would use drugs or alcohol to feel comfortable doing things my partner wanted (e.g., sexual acts). And/or I would pressure my partner into things until I got my way.

Never ❖ Rarely ❖ Sometimes ❖ Often ❖ Always

14. When angry, one or both of us would launch into a laundry list of criticisms.

Never ❖ Rarely ❖ Sometimes ❖ Often ❖ Always

15. One (or both) of us threatened to leave the relationship when we were upset.

Never ❖ Rarely ❖ Sometimes ❖ Often ❖ Always

16. If/when one of us had betrayed the other, such as breaking a promise, getting into secret debt, or cheating, there was an expectation that this betrayal was quickly "forgiven and forgotten."

Never ❖ Rarely ❖ Sometimes ❖ Often ❖ Always

17. One (or both) of us would give the other the silent treatment when upset. And/or one or both of us have "ghosted" the other at some point.

Never ❖ Rarely ❖ Sometimes ❖ Often ❖ Always

18. I felt increasingly numb, anxious, or depressed (hard time sleeping, constant exhaustion, isolating) in this relationship.

Never ❖ Rarely ❖ Sometimes ❖ Often ❖ Always

19. There has been physical aggression or violence in the relationship (pushing, hitting, shoving, choking, etc.).

Never ❖ Rarely ❖ Sometimes ❖ Often ❖ Always

20. One (or both) of us have secretly monitored the other person (e.g., placing a hidden camera in the home, putting an AirTag in their car, or stopping by their house unannounced to see if they're home or not).

Never ❖ Rarely ❖ Sometimes ❖ Often ❖ Always

21. One (or both) of us broke promises we made to the other person (e.g., paying money back, staying faithful, not drinking, or not changing hurtful behaviors like yelling).

Never ❖ Rarely ❖ Sometimes ❖ Often ❖ Always

22. One (or both) of us have shared intimate photos or videos of us without the other person's consent.

Never ❖ Rarely ❖ Sometimes ❖ Often ❖ Always

23. One (or both) of us would make fun of the other's appearance—age, weight, looks—and/or compare them negatively to other people.

Never ❖ Rarely ❖ Sometimes ❖ Often ❖ Always

24. One (or both) of us would call each other names.

Never ❖ Rarely ❖ Sometimes ❖ Often ❖ Always

25. One (or both) of us made threats to hurt or kill ourselves, loved ones (including pets), or each other if the other left the relationship.

Never ❖ Rarely ❖ Sometimes ❖ Often ❖ Always

26. I didn't feel safe with my partner (emotionally, physically, mentally, spiritually, financially, sexually).

Never ❖ Rarely ❖ Sometimes ❖ Often ❖ Always

27. Sexual consent was not respected in the relationship. When one of us wanted to have sex and the other didn't, the other person was pressured with force or emotional manipulation, such as pouting or the silent treatment.

Never ❖ Rarely ❖ Sometimes ❖ Often ❖ Always

28. When angry, one (or both) of us had thrown things such as a phone, punched walls, or physically blocked the other person from leaving the room.

Never ❖ Rarely ❖ Sometimes ❖ Often ❖ Always

Now take a moment to add up your scores. Calculate the points from Questions 1–12.

TOTAL = ________________

Never—0 points

Rarely—1 point

Sometimes—2 points

Often—3 points

Always—4 points

Now add up the points from Questions 13–18.

TOTAL = _______________

Never—0 points

Rarely—1 point

Sometimes—2 points

Often—3 points

Always—4 points

Now add up the points from Questions 19–28.

TOTAL = _______________

Never—0 points

Rarely—1 point

Sometimes—2 points

Often—3 points

Always—4 points

If your relationship scored 15 points or less, there were likely moments of stress or conflict where you and/or your partner may not have behaved as kindly or maturely as you'd like. This stress may have made you feel like things were toxic, but this score indicates that you may only need to make small adjustments in how you cope and approach relationships. Please complete this workbook, yet know that only certain skills and concepts may need special focus and attention to cultivate a securely attached relationship.

16–25 points—There were quite a few toxic relationship patterns that likely created a lot of stress at times. If you often felt like you couldn't quite figure out how to fix your relationship, that makes sense. Some of these patterns were likely so deep rooted and cyclical that they would be hard to overcome on your own. Know you are now doing the deep internal work necessary to interrupt these toxic patterns. This is what truly matters. Please take your time going through this workbook to cultivate the skills you need for a securely attached, healthy relationship. Remember that as you interrupt toxic patterns and change how you address relationship stress, you'll be much better equipped to attract—and maintain—a healthy relationship.

26–100 points—This is a toxic partnership that has likely been quite harmful to your overall sense of well-being and health. Right now, you may feel a lot of lingering self-doubt, pain, confusion, and embarrassment. This is understandable, as you've been through a very painful and intense experience. Please take your time as you go through this workbook and be gentle on yourself. You will heal in your own due time. It takes time to rebuild your well-being and to recover, but it's completely possible. Please stick with this process, being sure to soothe your emotions regularly (which you'll learn how to do shortly if you don't yet know how).

101+ points—This has been an extremely damaging and likely abusive partnership. Being honest about your situation takes tremendous courage. Take a moment to congratulate the internal strength it takes to be here right now. Looking how someone has mistreated you and/or how you've harmed someone else is a deeply emotional process. Given everything you've been through plus the courage it takes to complete this workbook, you may feel like you're on an emotional roller coaster. Know that you will recover with time, and you've already accomplished the first essential step: honesty. Take your time to complete the exercises in this workbook. There is no rush. Truly just by being honest and showing up here, you've made more progress than you may know right now. Finally, it is likely you may be carrying some trauma from this relationship. If this is the case, please seek the support of a trauma therapist (the Resources section in the back will help guide you to one).

Up until now, you've explored the workbook exercises from the perspective of Tylah. To assist you in exploring the various ways you may relate to the concepts you're learning, we will look at the upcoming exercises in this chapter from Nate's perspective.

• CASE STUDY: *Tylah and Nate*

Nate fell in love with how warm and attentive Tylah was when they met. But when their son was born, he started to feel completely ignored and dismissed. It seemed like Tylah only wanted him to pay the bills or for sex. When Nate would refuse sex because he was tired or wanted more connection, Tylah would pout and call herself "ugly." He felt like he couldn't win and would agree with her out of spite that she was unattractive now. He felt shut down and hopeless. When his coworker, Delia, started paying attention to him, Nate started to feel alive again. One thing led to another, and he found himself having a sexual relationship with her.

EXERCISE: Debriefing the Assessment

In the previous exercise, if you noticed—or validated—you were in a toxic relationship, you may feel overwhelmed or embarrassed. Thoughts of self-judgment like feeling "weak" or foolish are also common here. This is especially true if you are still with your partner. In this exercise, you will take some time to debrief the previous exercise. Journal about the following prompts:

1. What was your score? What do you think about this score? Does it feel right or off?

___

___

___

___

2. Did the assessment highlight any behaviors of your ex's or patterns in the relationship you didn't realize were toxic? Does this validate anything about how you felt?

___

___

___

___

3. What did the assessment highlight about how you treated your partner? What judgments arise, if any, about yourself based on this?

___

___

___

___

___

___

4. Who is to blame for the toxic relationship? Note: You are never responsible for abuse. Can you see how you (or your ex)—outside of abusive behaviors—were both responsible?

5. If somebody you love had the same relationship score you have, what feelings would you have for your loved one or about their relationship?

6. It's completely understandable that you were in a toxic relationship with such a score. The complex and valid reasons for this will be explored in upcoming chapters, but for now, can you try to comfort yourself? In chapter 1, you were self-validating. Can you validate finding yourself here right now?

Please know your honesty is incredibly brave! Hopefully, too, if you've doubted yourself about this relationship or leaving, this assessment and debrief validates that you did the right thing for you!

Example as Nate

1. My score was 133. I didn't know it was that toxic! No wonder I felt so shut down and angry.
2. I didn't realize that Tylah pouting when I didn't want sex was coercive and toxic. I just knew it made me feel gross. It makes sense now that it made me pull away from her more.
3. I realize that I was a lot more distant and mean than I wanted to admit. I was just so upset that she stopped caring about me, it seemed. I wanted her to show more interest in me, which I think is valid. But it wasn't okay for me to be mean to her or cheat on her.
4. Yeah, I thought Tylah was the main problem. But I guess I could've opened up to her without shutting down or cheating.
5. If somebody I cared about like my mom had this score, I'd feel angry and want them to leave.
6. Nate, it makes sense that this is the type of relationship you had with Tylah. After what you saw in your family growing up, I guess you didn't know any better.

The Toxic Relationship Cycle

All couples, whether the relationship is toxic or healthy, have familiar cycles of interacting. These cycles may be positive, such as establishing a seamless way you divide chores. Or these cycles may be painful or distressing, which is usually the case in toxic relationships. One common toxic relationship cycle is to have "off-limit" topics because they inevitably lead to fights when they're discussed, but partners bring them up anyway when they've reached their limit. Another common problematic cycle in toxic relationships is always sweeping things under the rug when there's conflict. This makes it so it never feels like anything is ever resolved or repaired. Often in toxic relationships, partners tend to blame one another for being the "real" problem in the relationship. However, when there is no abuse involved, it is the cycle that's to blame rather than either one person.

To fully recover from toxic relationship patterns, it's imperative to look at how you personally contributed to toxic cycles. This process of self-assessment is meant to be empowering. When you can see the way you may have contributed to gridlock or conflict in your relationship, you discover healthier options for your relationships moving forward. To break free from toxic patterns, you never need to wait for someone else to change. In fact, focusing on changing your own behaviors is the only way to ensure you fully recover rather than just hoping your next partner is "perfect" for you. There is nothing "wrong" with you if you noticed there were times when you contributed to toxic cycles. It's human to make mistakes and be imperfect. Additionally, when you consider your life experiences and potentially your relationship role models, these patterns of behaving make sense. You are not "bad" or the "problem." Rather, you are a human being who sometimes acts in ultimately unhelpful ways, *and* you are completely capable of changing.

For instance, when I was in my last toxic relationship, whenever I was disappointed, I would launch into a list of criticisms of my partner. I felt entitled to hurt him like this because he had hurt me. However, my roommate at the time explained I didn't have the right to do this. Rather, it was my responsibility to share my needs, but if he didn't want to meet them, it was also my responsibility to accept this. From this place, I could make the choice to accept the way he chose to treat me, since he wasn't willing to be more respectful, kind, or safe—or I could be more honest about my nonnegotiable needs. But instead, for years, I denied my needs. This made me feel "stuck" in this toxic relationship and I would criticize him as a way of getting unstuck. But ultimately, all I did was feed the toxicity between us. In the end, I eventually had to accept the truth that he may never be respectful or kind—and his track record alongside his lack of desire to change proved this would be an inevitability. This acceptance helped me stay away for good and become the source of my own liberation.

EXERCISE: Examining the Cycle

In this exercise, you will explore your role in reinforcing toxic cycles in your relationship. For instance, there may be ways you reacted to your partner or minimized reality that may have added to your pain. This helps you gain awareness as to which of your thoughts and/or actions contributed to your suffering in this relationship. This awareness allows you to envision new options for behaving that change your relationship cycles. Remember, this viewpoint is meant to empower you. You are *never* to blame for abuse; the person who abused you is always completely at fault for their choice to be abusive. This is true even when they gaslighted you as the reason they chose to harm you. You are never responsible for abuse *and* never deserve mistreatment.

1. Take a moment to review the previous assessment. Consider how your partner acted. Also, notice your own behaviors that may have been harmful. Write these here:

   Examples: I shut down and refuse to communicate. Or I'm kind of mean when I'm upset.

   ____

   ____

   ____

2. Now draw out the actual cycle of your toxic relationship to see it more clearly. To do this, alternate between what your partner would do or say with what you would do or say in response, and so on. You may feel free to add your emotions too. There's no right way to "start" this cycle—you can begin and end anywhere, as cycles repeat themselves. Try to map this like you were seeing the cycle as a fly on the wall, and without judgment.

   You may use the example below to help guide the map of your own cycle:

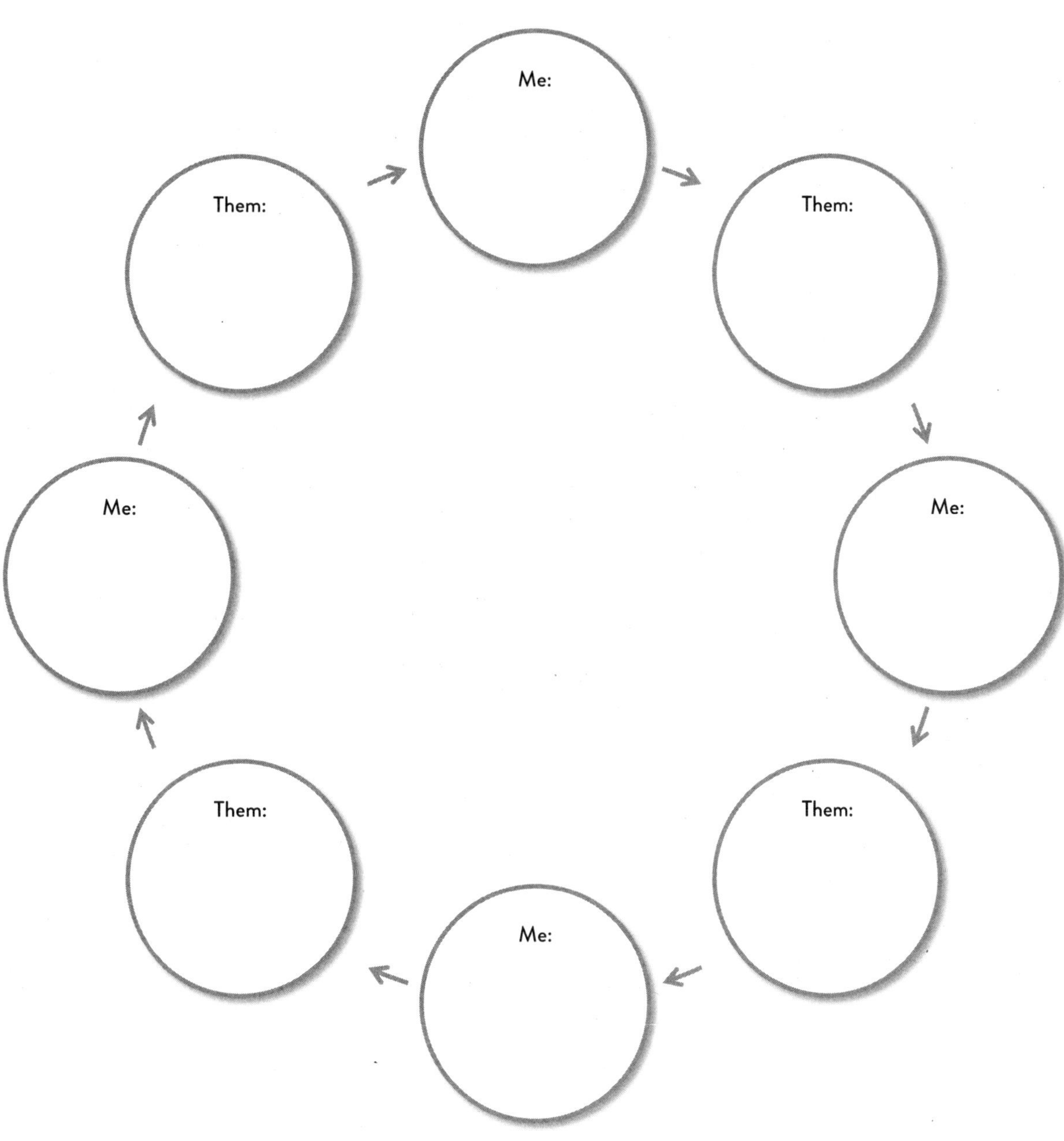
Me:
Them:
Me:
Them:
Me:
Them:
Me:
Them:

Example as Nate

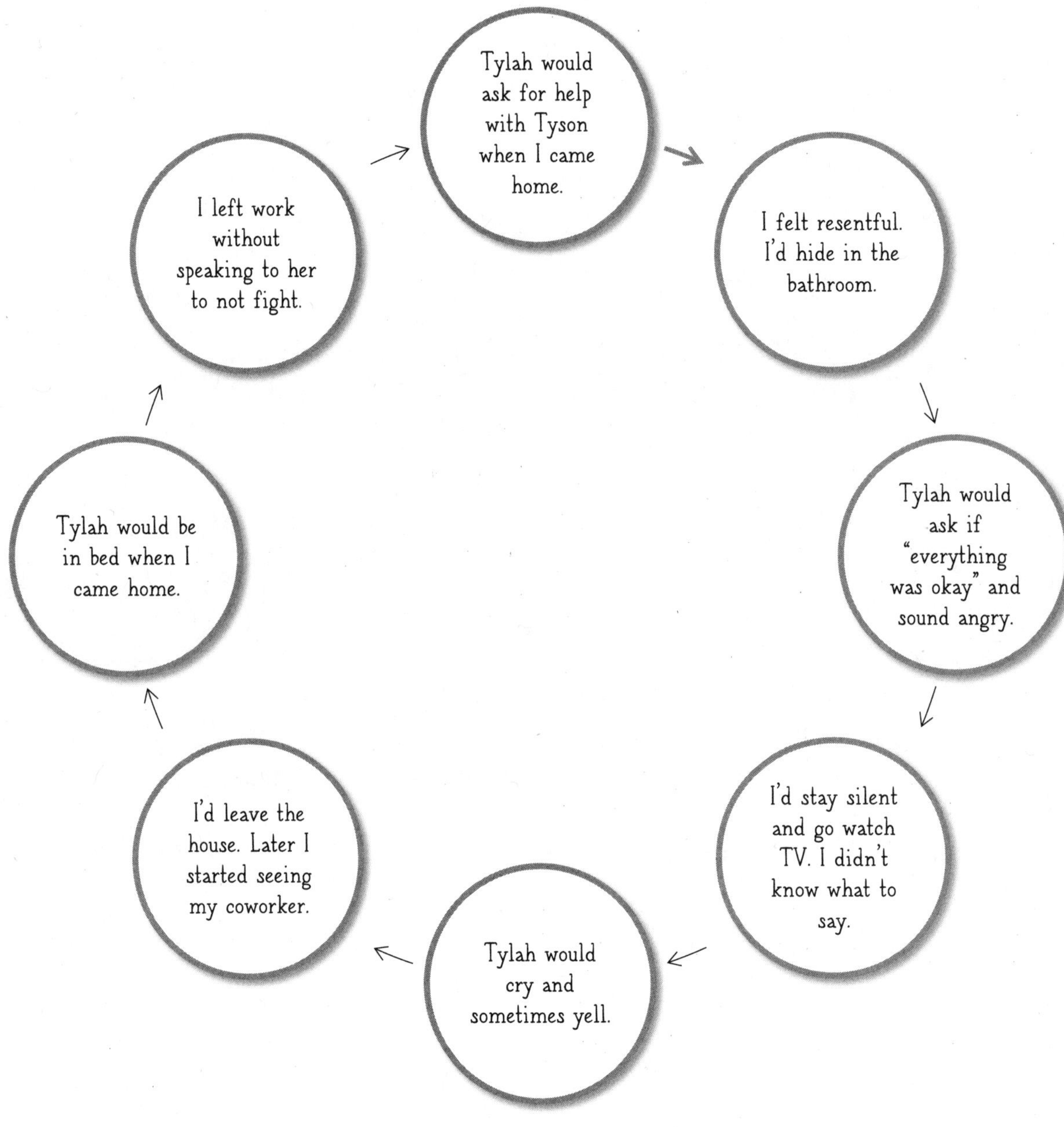

3. What do you notice when you consider the way your actions may have reinforced toxic interactions? Are you feeling defensive? Judgmental? Remember, you have been doing your best with the ways you've known how to cope and communicate.

4. If you're defensive and/or judging yourself, can you think about why these thoughts or behaviors make sense? What would you tell a good friend who had behaved in the same way?

   Example: It makes sense I shut down. My father did the same thing, and I learned men don't talk about feelings.

5. Now from a place of more compassion, identify one personal pattern of action that you can interrupt moving forward. You may not fully know *how* to do this yet, but you're planting important seeds of change by contemplating this.

   Example: Instead of shutting down, I can try to share when I'm upset, with kindness.

6. Plant a mental seed to be on the lookout for this pattern moving forward, as it may show up with other people. Remember, it's natural that you will still react in this way sometimes, *and* you can learn new ways of responding to others. This is what recovery is about—having old urges arise *while* choosing a new, healthier way to respond.

7. Create an action step for changing this pattern now. You may need to get creative, but anything that sounds like it will help you is the right answer!

   Example: I'll shut down less by speaking up more at work meetings when I have a question for now.

   ____

   ____

   ____

   ____

   ____

   ____

8. When this familiar pattern shows up, remember, it's not a failure. It's an invitation to try out your new way of thinking or acting. It's also an opportunity for self-validation, which is the process of being understanding with yourself while regarding your thoughts and feelings without judgment. Repeat this process as needed.

Defining Healthy Relationships

Your recovery road map requires knowing where you no longer want to stay as well as your goal destination. You recover by identifying, and changing, toxic relationship patterns. You also recover by knowing what a healthy relationship genuinely looks and feels like, to know you're headed in the right direction. To know your end goal, you create a healthy relationship template, learning more about what traits you want to cultivate in a relationship moving forward rather than only focusing on what you don't want to experience anymore.

Throughout this workbook, you'll be building your healthy relationship template. To start, let's look at some of the primary qualities of happy, long-lasting relationships proven by decades of research (Gottman 2011):

- Couples in happy, long-lasting relationships actively prioritize their friendship and intimacy. They make time for each other regularly because they genuinely love each other's company.
- They are willing to consider, and honor, their partner's point of view. They pay attention to what interests their partner and make time to share in conversations or activities that are meaningful to their partner.
- During disagreements, they practice empathy to get unstuck and find common ground to compromise effectively.
- They attack the problem, not each other, when there's conflict. They communicate as a team. Because of this sense of safety, they are able to stay regulated and calm with each other—as opposed to fighting, shutting down, placating, or running away from one another.
- They prioritize communicating and repairing when there are disagreements or setbacks. They successfully repair problems during the disagreement whenever possible, or take breaks and make sure to follow up if they need time to process their emotions.

Understandably, some of these qualities may have been limited in your toxic relationship. Right now, you may have questions arising about how to actually practice these things in a relationship. Throughout this workbook, you will learn how to be the type of partner capable of giving and receiving these healthy qualities with another.

EXERCISE: Envisioning a Healthy Relationship

Sometimes, especially early in recovery, we know we want our pain to end but we aren't sure whether anything more than that is possible. You may know you're done with toxic relationships, yet you may also be understandably skeptical at times about the possibility of having a healthy relationship. This may be especially true if you've had a lot of toxic relationships and/or saw a lot of toxic relationships growing up. This exercise helps expand your vision of what's possible for you to create. Please fill in the following pie chart in as much detail as possible to help you envision a positive future. An example is also provided to assist you in this brainstorming.

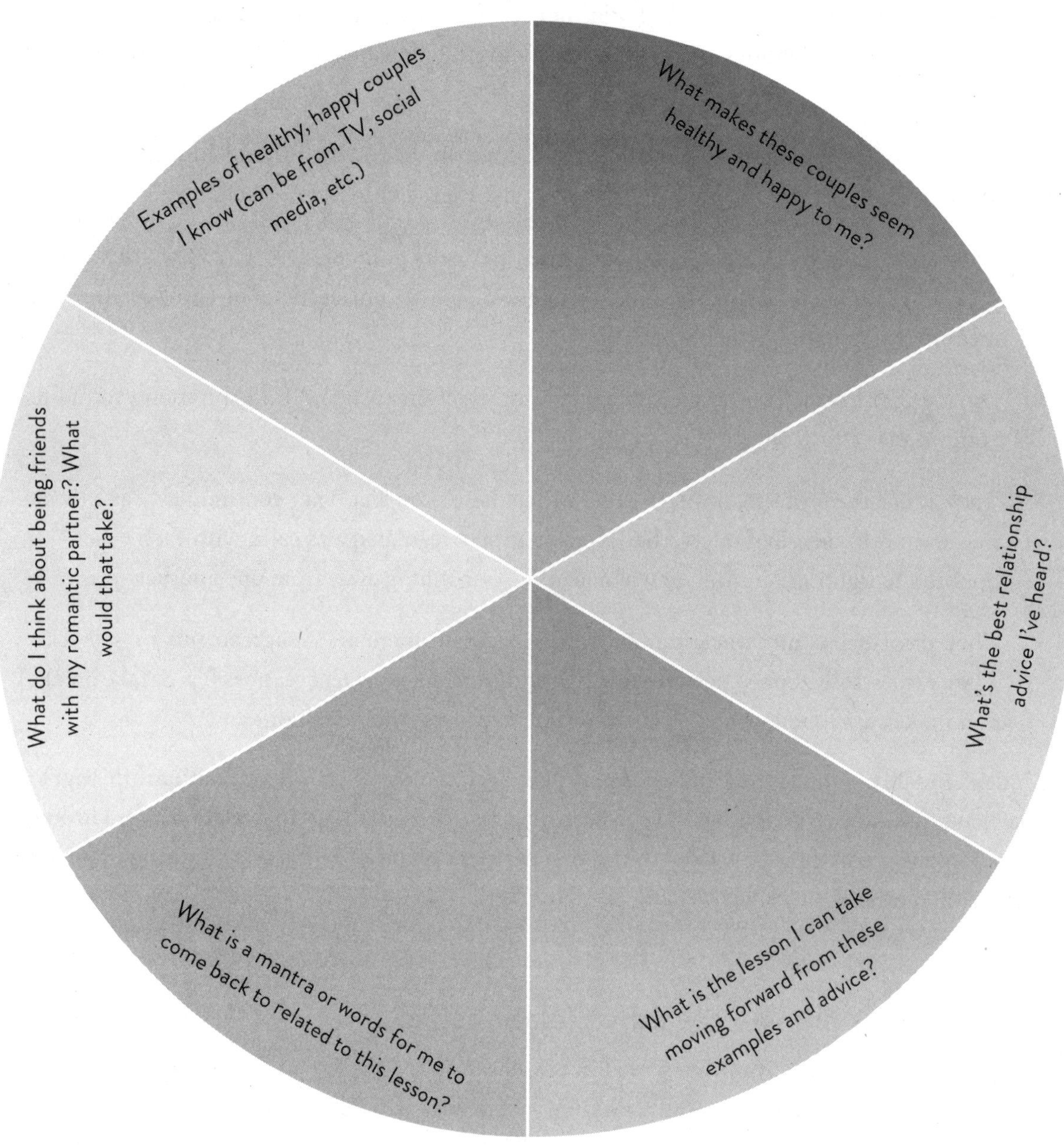
Examples of healthy, happy couples I know (can be from TV, social media, etc.)
What makes these couples seem healthy and happy to me?
What's the best relationship advice I've heard?
What is the lesson I can take moving forward from these examples and advice?
What is a mantra or words for me to come back to related to this lesson?
What do I think about being friends with my romantic partner? What would that take?

EXAMPLE AS NATE

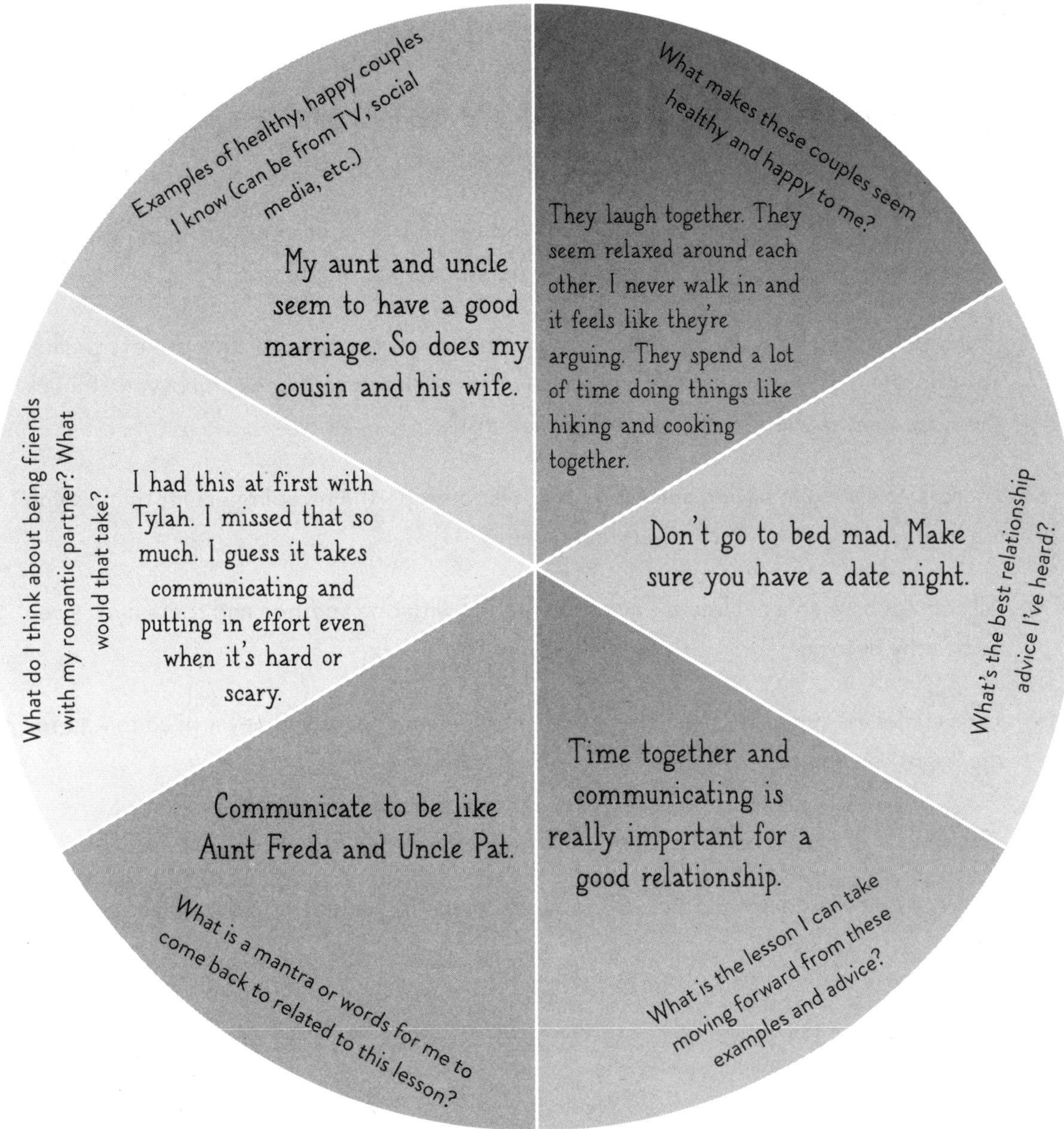

Moving forward, continue to look for proof that healthy relationships are possible. Explore the relationships you see around you for signs of the functional, healthy relationship qualities. Also, pay attention to signs that these traits may exist in people you find attractive. Finally, to help you break old patterns you identified in the previous exercise, come back to your mantra and lesson from this activity.

Toxic Relationships 101
Chapter Reminders

- Toxic relationships erode your well-being—this can include your mental, emotional, physical, financial, intellectual, spiritual, and/or sexual health.
- Some toxic relationships are also abusive—and the more abusive and damaging the relationship was, the more likely you may have developed trauma from it.
- If you developed trauma, consider attending trauma therapy to receive the extra care, attention, and support you may need as you go through this workbook and beyond (check the Resources section for help finding a therapist).
- There is no shame in having been in a toxic relationship—the most important thing is you are being honest now, which is very courageous.
- All couples have an established way of interacting with one another, and these cycles can be healthy or toxic.
- Toxic cycles are typically co-created by partners, which means you never need to wait for the "right" person to break free from toxic patterns now.
- You recover by changing the patterns within you that contribute to toxic dynamics.
- You recover by building your hope for and awareness of healthy relationship patterns.

Chapter 3

ATTACHMENT THEORY AND YOUR RELATIONSHIPS

You have courageously begun to explore the patterns in your toxic relationship, where you've been harmed and potentially where you've contributed to problems. Right now, you may feel lingering self-judgment for these cycles. Yet there is absolutely nothing wrong with you. Finding yourself entrenched in a toxic relationship is not your fault. Rather, it is a result of how you learned to form, and maintain, relationships in your life—your attachment style. Attachment theory explains how people show up in their relationships. Over fifty years ago, John Bowlby and Mary Ainsworth began to demonstrate that from birth, connection with others is a fundamental, nonnegotiable need (Bretherton 1992). When a baby is provided reliable, consistent connections with others, they grow into secure adults. They are able to have close relationships without losing themselves within them. They are able to tolerate the natural discomfort of vulnerability to deepen intimacy in their close relationships due to an internal sense of safety. At the same time, they know they are inherently worthy, and they don't tolerate mistreatment.

Sadly, when a baby or child doesn't have enough safe, reliable people or experiences in their life, this hurts their ability to feel safe within themselves and with others. They may struggle to trust in their inherent worth. They may also struggle to trust others or know how to discern who is trustworthy and who is not. This uncertainty and confusion is manifested as a nonsecure attachment style.

This theory of attachment is central to clarifying with compassionate understanding why you found yourself in a toxic relationship. Somewhere along the way, your ability to discern what's safe and unsafe became wounded. Your sense of self-worth may be wounded and/or your ability to trust others may have been eroded. You developed a nonsecure attachment style, which confused you around what you may deserve, expect, or demand from others. This is not your fault. At the same time, to fully recover from toxic relationships, you must heal your attachment style. Otherwise, people often just end up exchanging one toxic partner for another. You may have already experienced this before.

Healing your attachment style allows you to never feel "stuck" again in toxic relationship patterns. You fundamentally change the types of relationships you are willing to invest your energy in moving forward, as well as how you show up for others. There will, of course, still be potentially toxic partners out there, but you won't personalize this. No longer will you feel you must prove yourself or control others to receive the love we all inherently need. By becoming securely attached, you approach relationships with grounded, centered clarity and safety. You honor your inherent right to safety and consistency while respecting others' rights as well. Once here, your relationships with others become a source of joy and inspiration, rather than the cause of much of your suffering, as they may currently be.

Attachment Styles

There are four main attachment styles:

- Secure
- Anxious
- Avoidant
- Anxious-Avoidant (sometimes called "disorganized" or "fearful avoidant")

In *Attached: The New Science of Adult Attachment and How It Can Help You Find—and Keep—Love,* authors Amir Levine and Rachel S. F. Heller explain that just over 50 percent of people are securely attached. This means about half of people have an anxious, avoidant, or anxious-avoidant attachment style. They explain that 20 percent of people are anxiously attached while 25 percent are avoidant. Finally, 3 to 5 percent of people have an anxious-avoidant style (2010). Therefore, if you have a nonsecure attachment style, you are not alone and it's not your fault. Furthermore, *you can heal.*

Secure Attachment

A secure attachment style allows a person to create and maintain close, safe, and warm relationships with ease. They can read other people's cues accurately and make adjustments to their behaviors as needed. For instance, if someone appears bored when they're telling a story for a long time, they will wrap the story up to reengage without experiencing shame. They participate in the imperfect yet deeply important dance of human connection skillfully. This skill allows securely attached people to have many positive experiences with others. This, of course, becomes a positive cycle. Since connecting with others feels primarily fun and safe, they engage in positive ways with others, which continues to give them positive feedback. This continues to deepen their sense of joy and safety connecting with others.

Securely attached people are not only well attuned to others' cues but also to their own. They pay attention to their emotions and needs and care for them effectively. They can self-soothe appropriately, but when they need help from others (as we all do), they can ask for help without too much embarrassment or anxiety. They trust that others can be reliable and responsive to them. At the same time, they know other people will naturally make mistakes at times. They prioritize repairing the relationship when there is hurt or disappointment. They don't expect perfection—or sweep things under the rug.

Finally, a person with secure attachment trusts in themselves. They know they have a lot to offer others. They know they deserve respect, kindness, and safety from others as a bare minimum. As such, they tend to be much more responsive to "red flags" in their relationships because they have a much lower willingness to accept abuse or mistreatment from others. However, please note that there are many forms of abuse and mistreatment that are difficult to detect, such as gaslighting. A person with secure attachment can still enter, and maintain, a toxic relationship when they aren't aware of certain problems. Then over time, due to their partner's abuse, they can develop an insecure attachment style, which makes it harder and harder to leave the toxic relationship.

This workbook is your guide to cultivate or deepen your secure attachment, which is the best way to fully recover from toxic relationship patterns. Here, you will be equipped to self-protect from mistreatment appropriately while showing up intimately and vulnerably with others who are safe as well.

Anxious Attachment

A person with anxious attachment craves closeness and intimacy. They tend to be highly uncomfortable being single and will often rush from one partner to the next. A common way this manifests is the person who has never been single since they first began dating. Sometimes, they may even line up a new partner while leaving their current one. As they are afraid of being alone, they are often very fearful of being rejected, even for small mistakes. This leads them to sometimes fall into people-pleasing and perfectionism patterns. Here, they hope if they figure out how to perfectly make their partner happy, they can prevent abandonment.

Deep down, a person with anxious attachment often questions their authentic worth. They may fixate on being "chosen," even by a partner who is objectively unavailable, as a means to prove their worth. Rather than investing in available, mutually compatible partnerships as a securely attached person does, an anxiously attached person has equated love with something they have to earn.

Furthermore, a person with anxious attachment also often has a scarcity mindset around connection. They often believe it's extremely difficult, and rare, for them to find connections with others. Because of this, in a toxic relationship, they may be more willing to accept crumbs of attention or kindness rather than experiencing the "nothing" they perceive as the alternative. They will also question their needs. They may often wonder if their desire for basic respect or consistency is "too much" due to their low perceived value. Understandably, because of these insecurities alongside their fear of being alone, people with an anxious attachment style can find themselves stuck in toxic relationship patterns.

Avoidant Attachment

Despite the fact it's called avoidant attachment rather than anxious, a person with this attachment style is also afraid. While an avoidantly attached person still wants connection, as this is a core human need, they also fear closeness. This internal conflict leads them to frequently send mixed signals. A common example is a person who seems genuinely engaged for a few dates but then explains they're "too busy" for anything serious right now. However, they may still continue to try to see the other person casually. If they're dating an anxiously attached person, they can continue this dance for a long time. This is a very common toxic relationship pattern.

The excuse of being busy is just one way an avoidantly attached person pushes their partner away. A person with an avoidant attachment style primarily focuses on ways to keep others at a distance rather than nurturing intimacy. This is rooted in various fears, including the fear that intimacy will rob them of the freedom they greatly value or that others will suffocate, use, or manipulate them. Other common ways they create distance besides burying themselves in work or school include an unwillingness to "label" a relationship, cheating, and addictions to things like pornography or video games. Boundaries are important for healthy relationships, yet for a person with this attachment style, their boundaries often become impenetrable walls.

A person who has avoidant attachment may also be very critical of their partner (or ex-partners) as a way of creating distance. They are frequently "on guard" to any perceived threats to their independence or control. This pattern of criticism, coupled with their fear of losing their independence and their intense discomfort with vulnerability, leads them to end relationships more quickly than those with other attachment styles. Often, this happens without discussing things with their partner, as a person with this attachment style *avoids* intimate conversations. This can lead to them cutting people off suddenly or ghosting them. Finally, these individuals tend to be distanced from their feelings, so they "get over" people more quickly than others as well. All these patterns, of course, lead to an increased likelihood of finding themselves in toxic relationship cycles.

Anxious-Avoidant Attachment (or Disorganized)

Less commonly, a person may develop both an anxious and an avoidant attachment style. This attachment style can be extremely confusing for both the person with this style and their partner. This is because they have two profound yet conflicting fears around connection with others. Their anxiously attached part craves connection and is terrified of being alone, yet their avoidantly attached side makes them terrified of losing their freedom. They fear abandonment *and* intimacy. This inner conflict within the person understandably often leads to toxic relationship cycles.

As they have two conflicting parts, people with this attachment style may swing to extremes in relationships and run hot and cold. One moment, they may be affectionate and talking about future plans with someone. But the next, they may suddenly tell their partner, "It's not the right time for a relationship" or ghost them. This is a very painful cycle for both people in the relationship. Their partner is naturally left confused, often wondering who the "real" version of the person is. For the person with the disorganized attachment, their conflicting behaviors may reinforce their anxiously attached part's belief that they are "bad" or "less than." Due to this self-perception, sometimes they may even think they are doing others a favor by pulling away after becoming more intimate, a belief that also feeds into their avoidant part.

This disorganized attachment style may contribute to choosing unavailable or avoidantly attached partners. The person's anxiously attached part may want the validation of "proving their worth" to this person and being "picked." At the same time, they may find comfort in the distance provided by an unavailable partner because deep down, their avoidant part also doesn't want too much closeness. This latter part is often unconscious until a person begins to explore their toxic relationship habits. On the surface, they may feel obsessed with getting commitment with the unavailable person. Yet if they do get this commitment, their inner conflict may manifest as suddenly losing interest in this person. An anxious-avoidant attachment style most clearly looks like a pattern of self-sabotage in relationships.

EXERCISE: Assess Your Own Attachment Style

This assessment will assist you in clearly identifying your current attachment style. It's okay to be wherever you are right now. This exercise aims to empower you with self-awareness. By being aware of your current attachment style, you are better equipped to notice when nonsecure thoughts, urges, or actions arise. This conscious awareness helps you interrupt these old ways of being to make better choices.

Read each statement and circle any that feels true at least half of the time:

1. When my partner seems agitated, I automatically think they must be upset with me.
2. When I send someone I'm dating a text, I will fixate on how long it takes them to reply.
3. Sometimes I feel like a burden and that others are doing me a favor by sticking around.
4. I put up with how my partner (or ex) treats me because having this relationship is better than having nothing at all.
5. I'm afraid of being alone and hate being single.
6. At times, it feels like I cannot get close to someone I love even when we're in the same room.
7. It would feel like my life would end if my romantic relationship ended. (Or it felt like my life would end when my relationship ended.)
8. When someone hurts me, I tend to give them second, third, and even more chances to try to treat me better.
9. It feels like my partner (or ex) is the last person I'll ever feel connected to deeply.
10. I spend a lot of time thinking and talking about my partner (or ex).
11. If I see my partner on their phone or another device, I immediately worry they're cheating on me.
12. After I spend time with someone, or go on a date, I obsess about what I did or said that was wrong or embarrassing.

13. I avoid conflict at all costs, even if it means sweeping hurtful things under the rug.
14. The main problem in my relationships is that I'm too needy.
15. When someone mistreats me, I tend to empathize more with why they hurt me rather than caring about my own pain.
16. With all my responsibilities and interests, it's hard for me to make time for a relationship.
17. I have a hard time not blaming my partner (or ex) for all the relationship problems.
18. When I'm single, I fantasize about being in a relationship, but as soon as I'm dating someone, I fixate on their flaws and why we should break up.
19. The best way to get something done is to do it yourself.
20. It seems like no matter who I date, eventually they become too needy or clingy.
21. When someone really wants to get to know me, I feel repelled or disgusted.
22. I have a pattern of lying to the people closest to me.
23. I resent others needing, wanting, or expecting things from me.
24. I like a lot of space and alone time. Seeing someone more than once a week or two feels like too much.
25. It feels easier to be single than in a relationship.
26. I have betrayed or cheated on someone I cared for and even wanted a future with.
27. When problems arise in my relationship, I tend to isolate and withdraw.
28. I'm quick to cut people off or ghost them.
29. Even people who have known me a long time have told me I'm hard to get to know.
30. I tend to second-guess others' opinions and believe I do things the "right way."
31. I value consistency and reliability in a relationship.
32. There's a lot of warmth in my relationships and I trust in people's care for me.
33. I truly can see the value I bring to someone's life—I'm a good person to have around!
34. Overall, I feel proud of how I treat myself and others even when I'm emotional.

35. While communication is important, how someone treats me is more important than what they say.

36. I'm comfortable with depending on others when I need support.

37. I trust myself to see—and honor—red flags in the people I meet.

38. I know people make mistakes and I can forgive, yet if someone keeps hurting me, I'll set the boundaries I need to protect myself.

39. It's natural to get more attached to someone after having sex with them, so I take my time getting to know someone before having sex.

40. I'm comfortable having time apart from my partner to invest in other relationships and hobbies, but quality time is also important to maintain a good relationship.

41. When I have a problem or concern with someone, I can be direct and honest in a kind way, in the hopes of repairing the issue.

42. When someone I'm dating shows they aren't interested in me or in having a relationship, I will walk away even if it hurts, since I know what I'm looking for is available.

43. I'm comfortable letting people get to know the real me.

44. When someone hurts me, or leaves me, I know this isn't a sign that I'm less worthy than anyone else.

45. I'm comfortable committing to someone I like and fully investing my time and energy in developing the relationship.

How many statements did you circle for numbers 1–15? ________________

How many statements did you circle for numbers 16–30? ________________

How many statements did you circle for numbers 31–45? ________________

Statements 1–15: Anxious Attachment

1–5 points: You have some natural insecurities or fears that come up when you connect with others. This is completely natural and a part of being human. The important thing is you don't allow these fears to dominate your relationship with yourself or others.

6–10 points: You exhibit a pattern of anxious attachment. You may be preoccupied with your relationships and uncomfortable being on your own. To avoid being alone, these feelings may make you feel stuck in toxic relationships. As you use this workbook, please provide extra care to these scared and insecure parts of yourself to become more comfortable being with yourself.

11 or more points: You have an anxious attachment style. You may have felt stuck in toxic relationship patterns out of a sense that you aren't worth more kindness or respect. Or you may have been clinging to a partner you *know* isn't healthy for you because you're afraid of being alone or never finding another connection like this. Please be very gentle with yourself as you go through this workbook and develop more awareness of your true worth and the fact you deserve kindness and respect at the bare minimum.

Statements 16–30: Avoidant Attachment

1–5 points: You may sometimes worry about losing your independence in a relationship. This fear may manifest as occasionally being critical about your partner or isolating. Overall, though, you are able to cope well with these fears as they don't rule your perspective. Likely, you are able to still provide your partner with time, attention, and care in a balanced way.

6–10 points: You exhibit a pattern of avoidant attachment. Your fears around others needing or controlling you lead to a habit of distancing yourself from them. This prevents you from cultivating the intimacy you desire deep down. Going through this workbook, please pay attention to the parts of you that feel suffocated or overwhelmed when others want to be close to you or need something from you.

11 or more points: You have an avoidant attachment style. You may find yourself putting up walls with others by being critical, busy, or cutting people off to protect your independence and sense of self. You likely avoid intimate conversations and perhaps feel agitated when people want to know you more deeply. Sadly, this pattern keeps you stuck in toxic cycles where you find yourself engaging and then pulling back over and over from the closeness you most deeply desire. As you go through this workbook, please be compassionate with yourself as you learn to care for these scared and conflicted parts. You can heal and discover you are able to remain an independent person while being in a close relationship.

Statements 31–45: Secure Attachment

0 points: You don't yet have a foundation for a secure attachment style. That's okay. Likely, this hasn't yet been taught or role modeled for you. This workbook will help you plant seeds to develop a secure attachment style.

1–5 points: You have thoughts, feelings, or actions that reveal the seeds of a secure attachment style. This is truly a celebration! You will grow your secure attachment style from the seeds with this workbook.

6–10 points: You are well on your way to a secure attachment style. Allow yourself to feel the relief of noticing you simply have to grow this part up a little more while taming any nonsecure parts of self, which this workbook will guide you to do step by step.

11 or more points: Yay! You have a secure attachment style. While human relationships are complex, this attachment style most easily lays the foundation for a healthy, respectful, safe, and intimate, long-lasting relationship. You are encouraged to make future relationship choices from this securely attached part of yourself. This choice allows you to break free of toxic patterns once and for all.

Note: You may have multiple attachment styles. This is completely okay! People and relationships are complex and multilayered. If you have both avoidant and anxious parts, take your time with this workbook to complete the exercises. Honor both of these parts to help resolve your inner conflicts. This guides you toward a sense of wholeness and security within yourself—the foundation of secure attachment! Also, if you have both a nonsecure *and* a secure attachment style within you, remember to make your choices moving forward from the secure part to fully recover.

• CASE STUDY: *Josue and Lara*

Lara and Josue have been married for five years. Lara's been dropping hints more and more that she's ready to have a child. Josue will laugh it off or sometimes say he just needs more time. Additionally, Lara does all the cooking and cleaning for the couple, and if dinner isn't done "on time" or there's a mess, he'll complain that she won't be able to be a good mom if she can't keep up already. Lara becomes terrified that he'll make her wait even longer to become a mom, so she fixates on being the "perfect" wife—like Josue's mom. After some time though, Lara became burned out and began resenting Josue for being a "child." She criticizes him for not growing up and that it's time to be a father—his parents already had two kids by his age. Josue becomes defensive at this and blames Lara for their childlessness, saying that he can't have kids with someone who is so "crazy." They end up screaming at each other until Josue leaves to go drinking. The next day, they don't address their concerns and have makeup sex, promising never to fight again.

EXERCISE: Rewriting a Story from Your Past

For this exercise, consider a past event or situation where your anxious or avoidant attachment style may have contributed to your current problems. For instance, maybe out of a fear of being alone, you ignored "red flags" when you met your ex. Or maybe when you fought with your ex, you fixated on how they were to blame without ever taking accountability for your role. You will rewrite the past by considering a new story of how you would have acted in that same situation if you had been more securely attached.

The goal of this exercise is to plant seeds for how to act from a place of secure attachment. This is not to blame or shame yourself; you have done the best you can with your current tools and skills. Try to give yourself understanding. Remember, the most important thing is that you are showing up for yourself now to truly change and grow.

1. What was a past relationship event that highlighted your current attachment style? Describe the situation, including how you thought, felt, and acted.

____

____

____

____

____

____

2. In the same situation, if you were securely attached and the anxious and/or avoidant part of you was managed successfully, how might you have responded? Note the ways you may have thought, felt, or acted from a securely attached place.

____

____

____

____

____

____

Example as Lara

1. When Josue tells me I won't be a good mom, I focus on trying to prove myself. This highlights my anxious attachment style.
2. From a securely attached perspective, when Josue complains that dinner isn't on time or there's a mess and says I won't be a good mom, I'd let him know how much this hurts my feelings. I'd ask him to contribute more to our household chores to prepare for our family, as there will be too much work for any one person to manage anyway when we have a kid.

Awesome job! Just by contemplating how you could act differently in familiar situations, you direct your life in a healthier way. The seeds of secure attachment sprout from simply contemplating this new way of being! Now to close this chapter, let's build on your hope for the future.

EXERCISE: Visualizing Your Securely Attached Future

It may be hard, at times, to see all the possibilities your recovery journey holds for you. Your primary focus may be to get out of suffering, which is an honorable goal. Yet to stay motivated—especially when the recovery work feels challenging—it's helpful to stay connected to your "big picture." In chapter 1, you created a pie chart envisioning your life once you've recovered. To expand on this, you will consider one area in your life that's calling you to make a change. This may be finally blocking your ex or going to therapy as examples. In this activity, you will see how this one change may lead to ever-expanding positive change and growth. By blocking your ex, you may notice that this gives you the space to fully recover. This then allows you to be much more present to dating in healthy ways, which paves the way for you to find your right partner. This then allows you to experience the joy of a long, happy relationship with a true friend.

This activity isn't about reading the future, of course. It's simply an invitation to consider the next logical step, should you take the next right action as a person who is recovering. In the image of the staircase below, put the change *you know* is nagging at you on the bottom step. Then notice how this change will lead to different positive stages by marking it on each advancing step. See the example from Lara for extra support.

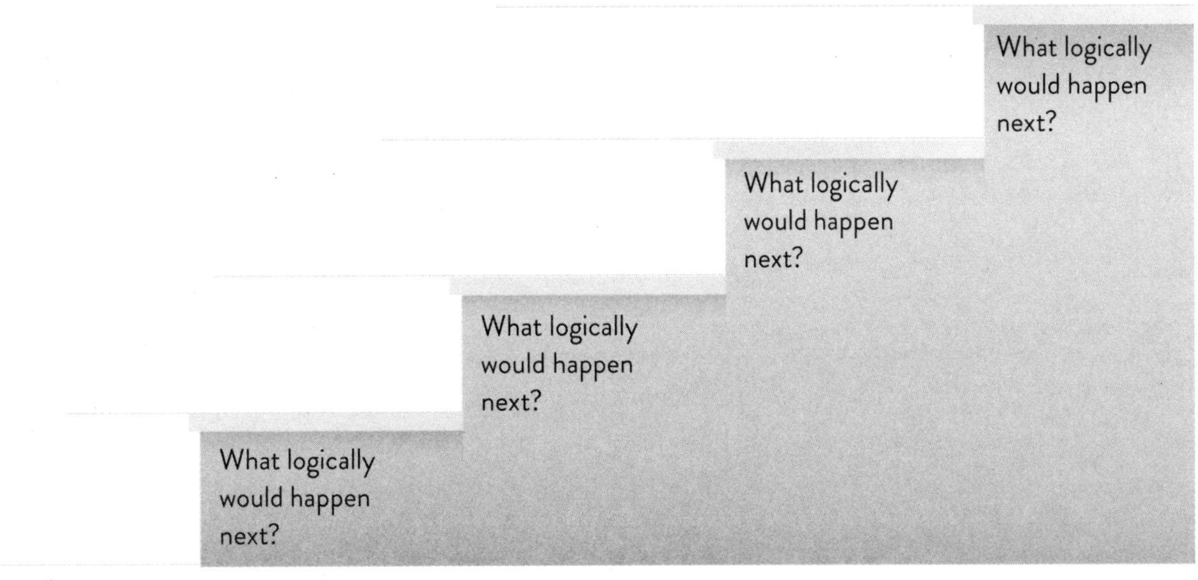

First change

Example as Laura

I'd have the confidence to finally ask Josue if he genuinely wants to have kids—or not. And have the confidence to make the changes I need if he doesn't want to be a parent. I can't give this up.

What logically would happen next?

I would stop feeling so much pressure to be "perfect" for Josue as I'm more confident.

What logically would happen next?

I'd probably start to feel good in my body again and like myself more.

What logically would happen next?

I'd start going to dance classes again.

What logically would happen next?

Stop doing all the chores.

First change

Wonderful job! You are already making fantastic gains toward this future (even if you can't see it yet). Step by step, your life will change. Initially, this will likely feel like a slow process. However, one day you will wake up and see you really did change the entire trajectory of the whole rest of your life when you committed to your recovery!

Attachment Theory and Your Relationships Chapter Reminders

- Attachment theory explains how people form and maintain close relationships, whether these are healthy or toxic.
- There are four attachment styles: anxious, avoidant, anxious-avoidant, and secure.
- All nonsecure attachment styles contribute to toxic relationship problems, as these impact how you see yourself, how you see others, and how you feel about intimacy.
- You anxious and/or avoidant parts are not the enemy—it's better to mindfully care for them rather than "fighting" them.
- In recovering from toxic relationship patterns, you are simply growing the securely attached part of you (even if you're starting from the ground up).
- Every time you stay patient with yourself and stay committed to this workbook and your recovery, even when it's uncomfortable, you are becoming more securely attached!

Chapter 4

BECOMING SECURELY ATTACHED

All human beings need connection with others. To be truly healthy and happy, this is a nonnegotiable need. At times, though, our culture minimizes this need. Worse, this literal need for connection, belonging, and support is sometimes pathologized as weakness or codependency. However, we need others to survive and thrive.

Living without close connections to other human beings is literally painful and toxic. Research shows lonely people hurt both emotionally *and* physically. Lonely people are much more likely to have anxiety or depression than people who have close connections (Batanova, Weissbourd, and McIntyre 2024). Furthermore, loneliness impairs the immune system, disrupts sleep, and contributes to higher levels of the stress hormone cortisol (Yanguas, Pinazo-Henandis, and Tarazona-Santabalbina 2018). Over time, these higher levels of cortisol are linked with high blood pressure, which increases someone's chances of heart attack and stroke (American Heart Association 2024). With the health risks associated with loneliness, researcher Julianne Holt-Lundstad found social disconnection is as harmful to our health as smoking fifteen cigarettes a day (2021).

Despite these facts, you may currently judge your need for human connection negatively. To support your recovery, though, try to remember this essential truth: We need other people to be truly healthy and happy. This is true even if your toxic relationship history or attachment style has obscured the fact. In reality, your toxic relationship history proves this need is fundamental. You have still tried to connect deeply to another person even as your nonsecure attachment style hasn't fully equipped you to do this in a way that feels truly nourishing.

If you have an anxiously attached part, you may find it easier to be more compassionate toward yourself when you consider the importance of human connection. This anxiously attached part is acutely aware of the dangers of social isolation and disconnection. From this lens, doesn't it make sense that you may have clung to someone who only gave you crumbs, deciding that this was better than nothing at all? You have been trying to receive the benefits of human connection—even if has ultimately been in a toxic situation that hurt.

And hopefully, with this information, you can also be gentler with yourself if you have an avoidant attachment style. It makes sense that while a part of you feels safer or less encumbered being alone, you have still felt compelled at times to have intimate relationships. Your internal conflict highlights a part of you that knows it's necessary to connect with others to be truly healthy and happy.

Wherever you currently find yourself, know that your recovery work is some of the most important self-care you can provide yourself in your lifetime! As you heal your attachment style, you are more equipped to receive the mental and physical health benefits of close, safe relationships without internal conflict or suffering.

Safety and Attachment

While we are hardwired to connect to others, we also have a primal drive as humans to stay safe. When securely attached, we clearly understand *and feel* the truth that safety comes from close, respectful relationships. Yet sometimes the cues to what's safe—and dangerous—with others can get confused in our hardwiring.

Our nervous system is designed to protect us from threats to ensure our survival. We have two fundamental parts of our nervous system. You may be familiar with the "fight-or-flight response," which comes from our sympathetic nervous system. Here you react to danger by either running away or fighting to protect yourself. When this system is overwhelmed and you feel shut down, this is the "freeze" state. Then, once you are safe, your parasympathetic nervous system is activated, which is also referred to as the "rest and digest" state. Here you can fully relax, sleep well, and your body can heal itself—and connect with others with ease and joy.

Ideally, and when working optimally, the state of our nervous system and risk are aligned. This means we are able to accurately assess if we are in danger or safe. When you're securely attached, once you've assessed this, you are able to take the necessary actions to either protect yourself or engage in the relationship. (Remember, though, some forms of abuse are so covert that it may be difficult to identify them until your sense of security has been shattered.)

However, these cues as to what's safe and what's dangerous often become confused when you have a nonsecure attachment style. An anxious attachment style often leads people to not appropriately respond to threats to their well-being. A person may give someone endless chances to disrespect them with this attachment style. Of course, this erodes their sense of self-esteem. But acting from their anxiously attached part, they prioritize their fear of being alone over how they're literally being harmed. On the other hand, an avoidantly attached person may find themselves wanting to flee from healthy emotional intimacy. They've confused healthy yet perhaps uncomfortable intimacy and vulnerability with danger.

Clinician Deb Dana calls these reversed reactions to threat and safety "misattunement" (2018). It's this misattunement that helps explain your anxious or avoidant reactions to others. Looking through this lens, you may see that your anxious or avoidant reactions are trying to keep you safe—even if they're not authentically aligned with the situation. Your anxious part is reacting more to the sense of danger in not being connected to a partner. On the other hand, your avoidant part is trying to protect you from intimacy, which sometimes *feels* dangerous.

EXERCISE: Responding with Attunement When You Feel Threatened

Resolving any misattunement you may have around safety and risk when engaging with others helps you become securely attached. Once you consciously explore what's underlying a sense of being threatened in a relationship, you may explore if this response is accurate to the situation. Your sense of fight, flight, or freeze may be triggered in relationships by a number of things, including a sense of being abandoned or rejected. It may also get triggered by conflict or when you feel your independence is under attack.

In this exercise, you will identify at least one time you felt overwhelmed, scared, or suffocated in a relationship. You'll also consider how you reacted at the time, perhaps from your nonsecure attachment style. Then you'll go deeper with what's making you feel threatened or scared to build insight about the insecurities underlying how you reacted. Finally, you'll consider how you would respond to the same threat if you acted in a securely attached manner. For support in moving through this exercise, please see the examples provided.

When did I feel threatened? (overwhelmed, scared, rejected, abandoned, suffocated, wanting to run or fight)	My response? (anxious, avoidant, or both)	What am I most scared of?	How would I have responded if I acted securely attached?
Lara: I'm scared Josue doesn't want kids with me. I'm afraid he thinks I'll be a bad mom.	I try to prove I'm the perfect wife to make him know I'll be a good mom. (anxious)	I'm terrified he'll leave me and I'll never get to have kids. I'll die alone.	I would tell him directly how important having kids is to me in my life—that I can't compromise on this. I'd ask him his true vision for the future rather than talking around it or fighting about it.
Josue: I'm suffocated by Lara's desire to have kids right now.	I criticize her cleaning or cooking and say I think she won't be a good mom. Or I distract and make jokes when she brings it up. Or I tell her it's not a good time for me. (avoidant)	I'm actually afraid I'll be a bad dad like mine. I would rather not have kids than act like my dad.	I'd tell Lara that my dad was physically abusive growing up. I'd tell her I get so scared of my anger and being my father's son—that's why I leave when we fight. I'd say I'm afraid I won't be able to control this part if we have kids.

When did I feel threatened? (overwhelmed, scared, rejected, abandoned, suffocated, wanting to run or fight)	My response? (anxious, avoidant, or both)	What am I most scared of?	How would I have responded if I acted securely attached?

Becoming Safe to Yourself

You are doing a wonderful job contemplating how you'd act in your relationships when you're securely attached. This lays the groundwork for acting in new ways in the moment. Right now, though, it's completely understandable if you find yourself uncomfortable with intimacy or clinging to relationships that hurt. While you will only invest in nourishing, safe relationships once you're securely attached, it takes time to get there.

The first step to truly having safe, intimate relationships with others is to learn how to show up *for yourself* as a safe person. Throughout this process, you are learning how to be a consistently safe and trustworthy person. This is the foundation of a healthy relationship when you're securely attached: You are a safe person both for yourself *and* for your partner.

To support and guide this process, the Internal Family Systems (IFS) therapy model, which was developed by Richard C. Schwartz (2023), is very helpful. This therapy model allows you to cultivate a secure attachment style *with yourself.* This is invaluable for recovering from toxic relationships. This secure attachment toward yourself allows you to protect yourself fully when others harm you without getting stuck in shaming or guilting yourself. This sense of deep-rooted safety inside of you also allows you to tolerate the discomfort of vulnerability to cultivate intimacy with a healthy partner.

IFS teaches that we all have different parts within us. Some of these parts we automatically react out of while others we suppress. Hiding, suppressing, or exaggerating these parts leads to emotional and relationship problems. However, while acting in an imbalanced way from these parts may cause problems, there are no parts of us that are "bad" or "wrong" (just like with our emotions). All of these parts aim to keep us safe, and yet they don't fully have the tools they need to effectively stay safe for ourselves and others all the time. For example, one part may tell us we have to micromanage everything to be okay, but this part also burns us out while causing resentment.

The goal of IFS is to cultivate and live from a sense of internal wholeness as your Self. Your Self is your true, wise, eternal essence that's always with you. Even if you can't sense it yet, which is completely understandable given the emotional roller coaster of toxic relationships, your Self is like the calm waters within you under the rocky waves of the noise and chaos of your current life. You may consider it your soul, your higher self, your internal light, or any other terminology that resonates with you as the core of who you are. It is your parts that have been wounded in life and now act in imbalanced ways to survive, which sadly perpetuates toxic relationships. Yet your inherent Self is already whole, wise, and unconditionally worthy.

Using the lens of attachment, your Self acts like a securely attached parent to all your parts—seeing them, understanding them, soothing them, and loving them unconditionally. To clarify, this is different than the parts of you that may have acted as nonsecure inner parents. For instance, when someone hurt you, a nonsecure inner parent may have cut them off or guilted you into staying quiet to try to survive. Rather, living from the Self is acting like a securely attached parent to yourself. Here, you would validate your pain without getting stuck in blame, shame, or judgment of yourself or others. Next, you would soothe yourself and then explore any needs from your various parts. Once your needs were identified, your Self would then honor these needs appropriately and attentively. For instance, you might speak to this person kindly but firmly to express your feelings and set limits to effectively protect your parts. Eventually, you are then able to have a securely attached relationship with someone else where you interact with each other from a place of Self-to-Self leadership, where you are safe for all your personal parts *and* all of their parts.

Your securely attached Self brings into harmony all your different parts without judgment. This includes your anxious and/or avoidant parts. They are not bad, but rather developed to help you feel safe, even if they ultimately create more problems than they help address. When you accept your parts, you stop fighting your anxious and/or avoidant urges. These parts are not the enemy; instead, they are parts of you that are hurting. As we build the secure part of you—this whole, securely attached Self—you can compassionately and effectively help your nonsecure parts. This creates a secure base within yourself so that no matter what happens in your relationships, you maintain a sense of safe, grounded presence within your own being. You trust you will be okay no matter what, which means you can tolerate leaving relationships when they hurt you *and* show up for healthy ones even when it's uncomfortable. No one can take you away from your Self. Never again will you feel that a relationship robbed you of your sense of self—or has the power to suffocate or control you.

EXERCISE: Exploring Your Relationship with Yourself

Your relationship with yourself is the foundation for your relationship with all other people. Yet for many people with nonsecure attachment, their inner critic is a very loud part of them. This part may question your worth, believing you must constantly work to prove yourself. Or it may believe that you are worth so little you must cling to toxic relationships—and guilt yourself into silence. Maybe your inner critic projects a lot of criticisms onto others, believing that if only *they* would change, you could finally be okay. There is no shame in this, yet to best care for this critical part of you, it's important to consciously explore it. This is helpful in becoming safe for yourself *and* others because your self-talk is a powerful indicator of how safe others may feel with you too.

1. On a scale of 0–10, with 10 being unconditional self-love and acceptance toward yourself and 0 being the experience of always judging and criticizing yourself harshly, how would you currently rate your relationship with yourself? (Try not to judge this—wherever you are is okay and understandable.)

____

2. If you are not always loving and accepting toward yourself, this makes sense, as no one is perfect. Yet to build opportunities to deepen your self-love, what are some of the things you judge, criticize, or find

unacceptable about yourself? Think about what words you use to judge or criticize yourself, such as "lazy," "needy," or "weak." Write any of these words here to build awareness. Take breaks as you need.

3. Do you ever use these same words to judge others? If so, what comes to mind? Or are you more accepting of others for these same things? If so, what do you say to yourself when you see these traits or patterns in others? Do you ever use different words to judge or criticize others in your mind (or aloud)? Write any of these words here.

4. Pick one of these judging words you noted and list the ways it impacts your view of self, how close you are to others, and your mental and physical health.

Example as Josue

I get stuck in thinking myself or others are "bad." This includes things that aren't even happening, like how I'd be as a dad. Then I project this onto Lara, saying she'll be a "bad" mom. This makes us fight and I feel embarrassed. Then I get drunk. I'm too hungover in the morning to get much work done, which makes me feel like a "bad" employee. Then, I don't know how to open up to Lara about all of this, so I feel "bad."

Example as Lara

I call myself and others "lazy." Because of this, I never let myself take breaks or relax. I'm constantly exhausted. I also feel like I'm failing all the time because there's always more work to get done. I want to prove I'm good at everything and not lazy, so I never ask for help. But then I resent Josue for being "lazy." Sometimes, I think he's doing me a favor by not wanting to have kids because I don't want to be his mom too.

5. What are your automatic thoughts, feelings, and reactions to the idea that healing your toxic relationship patterns involves letting go of judging yourself harshly and cultivating more self-love?

____

____

____

____

6. Wherever you are currently about the idea of being kinder to yourself, that's okay. However, to support your recovery, is there anything you can do to interrupt your patterns of judgment and criticism? For example, maybe you don't know how to be nicer to yourself yet, but you could try not to gossip about others (this may include not leaving unkind comments on social media or following celebrity gossip).

____

____

____

____

You are doing a wonderful job shining light on your relationship with yourself. From this place, you are cultivating your securely attached part. Here, you know that you never need to "prove" your worth. The same is true for others. You, like everyone else in the world, are inherently worthy. Instead, there are things that work for you and things that don't. You move from judging things to discerning your needs, wants, and boundaries. Then you advocate for these things in clear, direct, kind ways from your securely attached place.

Becoming Loving to Yourself

In the last exercise, if you noticed that a part of you is uncomfortable with cultivating more self-love, you are not alone. When I was stuck in toxic relationship patterns, I resented how often the self-help I read emphasized self-love. Truthfully, I found it nauseating—and confusing. The idea that I didn't value myself when I had the confidence to pursue academic and professional goals didn't make sense. And yet, in my personal life, my choices repeatedly reflected how committed I was to self-destruction.

It took me a long time to recognize that my choice to date manipulative, unavailable, and sometimes abusive men reinforced a deep-rooted belief that I was "not good enough." This belief convinced me I needed to settle for crumbs—or else I'd get nothing at all. Over time, though, I realized that how these men treated me had *never* been about my worth or value. Rather, their treatment simply reflected what I allowed because of my lack of self-worth. To recover, I opened up to the idea of becoming more self-loving. Then, as I learned to have a healthier relationship with myself, the type of romantic relationship I invested my energy in changed for the better.

To recover from toxic relationship patterns, you must become more lovingly connected with all your parts. This focus on self-love may feel trite or cliché at times, and yet the truth remains that this is an essential recovery step. This is sometimes clearer if you have anxiously attached parts that may feel "less than" and are preoccupied with abandonment or rejection. You may mistakenly believe that someone else has the power to finally make you matter by choosing you romantically (or professionally). This "less than" feeling highlights a sense of disconnection from your inherent internal wholeness as your Self. This self-disconnection is inherently painful, *and* it hurts your relationships by putting too much pressure on other people. All human beings are inherently valuable yet imperfect. Therefore, no one can live up to the responsibility of making you feel whole when you don't feel this way. No one, no matter how loving they are, will ever be able to make you feel inherently valuable. This recovery work is up to you.

Avoidant parts are also disconnected from the inherently valuable, authentic Self, but this may be obscured. Research shows that while self-esteem is lowered the more anxiously attached someone is, there is not the same correlation for avoidant attachment (Set 2019). This may be because the way avoidantly attached people behave fits into the values of Western, individualistic society more than anxiously attached people (Emery et al. 2018). Avoidant parts tend to be more preoccupied with productivity and professional success, to the detriment of close relationships. Often this is due to a simultaneous discomfort with intimacy and a devaluation of the importance of close relationships for well-being (which is often reinforced by Western cultural narratives). These parts may mistakenly believe their worth is tied to their accomplishments *and* that when they are successful, they are "better than" others. The true Self knows, though, that you are neither inferior nor superior to others, regardless of your accomplishments, appearance, or bank accounts and so on. By learning how to feel your inherent and equal worth as your whole Self, you experience a true freedom. No longer is your sense of value resting on something as precarious as external validation.

Furthermore, if you have an avoidant part, you may have a fear of suffocation or self-annihilation if you connect deeply with someone. This fear of intimacy highlights self-disconnection. If you felt truly whole, you'd know no one can ever take you away from you. As you develop a securely attached sense of your core Self, you then learn to tolerate the discomfort of intimacy to receive its benefits, which we all need. While you may occasionally feel overwhelmed, from this more secure place, you would communicate rather than disappearing, and set healthy, flexible boundaries rather than building walls.

Your Complex Self

The idea of bringing all your parts into harmony with your whole Self acting as a securely attached parent may still sound a little odd, and that's completely okay. For now, you only need an open mind and a willingness to explore this in baby steps to recover. However, to highlight the truth that you have multiple parts, consider how you've probably experienced internal conflict around your toxic relationship at some point. For instance, a part of you may have known you needed to walk away, while another part of you was tremendously hopeful that your relationship could be fixed. Or maybe one part feels like your toxic partner was completely to blame, and another judges yourself as the sole problem. This internal conflict highlights that you have different parts of self.

Having these different, often conflicting parts of self is an aspect of being human. This is different from "multiple personality disorder," or its clinically accurate term, Dissociative Identity Disorder (DID). A key difference is you are typically aware, on some level, of hearing your different parts of self, like a part that wants to recover and a part that's skeptical. Yet a person with DID commonly has "amnesia" moving between parts; that is, one part genuinely doesn't know what they said or did when they were acting from another part (Saxena, Tote, and Sapkale 2023). If you suspect you have this amnesia at times, DID must be diagnosed by a mental health professional.

EXERCISE: Honoring Your Complexity

For this exercise, you will begin exploring your different parts. To start, please go back to the attachment assessment in chapter 3. Note here the score you received for these parts:

Anxious: ________________ **Avoidant:** ________________

For every part with a score of 1 or higher, please fill out the following prompts.

Anxious

1. Where does my anxious part show up in my life? With whom? What thoughts clue me in to being in my anxious part?

____

____

____

2. What are its triggers? List as many as you can think of.

____

____

____

3. What is my anxious part's biggest insecurity? What's its biggest fear?

____

____

____

4. What does my anxious part most desire?

____

____

____

5. Is there anything I can do differently to better care for my anxious part?

____

____

____

____

Example as Lara

1. My anxious part shows up mostly with Josue. I know I'm feeling anxiously attached when I start trying to figure out how to make Josue happy enough to have kids with me.
2. Triggers:
   - Seeing my friends having kids—and some now on to their second or third kids when I have none!
   - Seeing my mom who wants to be a grandma
   - When happy families come on TV
   - My period
3. My anxiously attached part's biggest insecurity is that if Josue doesn't want kids with me—when we have such a good connection—then no one would. I'm deeply worried that there's something inherently wrong with me.
4. I most desire to feel "good enough" for my dream of having a family.
5. Yes; when this part comes up, I can remind it that I'm worthy of having children. Josue's inability to commit to having children—when he promised me he wanted this before getting married—isn't about me. There's something going on with him and it's not my fault.

Avoidant

1. Where does my avoidant part show up in my life? With whom? What thoughts clue me in to being in my avoidant part?

2. What are its triggers? List as many as you can think of.

3. What is my avoidant part's biggest insecurity? What's it's biggest fear?

4. What does my avoidant part most desire?

5. Is there anything that I can do differently to better care for my avoidant part?

Example as Josue

1. My avoidant part comes up with Lara—and with my friends. I know I'm feeling avoidant when I am having a hard time or feeling overwhelmed, and I tell myself to keep it quiet.
2. Triggers:
   - Lara telling me she's ready to get off birth control
   - When she makes "hints" about kids
   - When her mom brings over baby stuff "just in case"
   - Seeing my mom and her relationship with my dad
3. My avoidant part is terrified of being like my dad, who was abusive.
4. I most desire having a happy family. I've always wanted to be the dad I didn't get!
5. Yes; when I feel avoidant and want to shut down, I can tell myself that things will only get better if I communicate openly with Lara.

Now, complete this section regardless of what your secure attachment score initially was. Some of these questions may require that you use your imagination. If you can't identify an answer after taking some time, please be understanding with yourself. Just the act of truly contemplating these prompts is an act of change.

Secure

1. Are there any times I feel securely attached? That I trust in my worth, while also trusting that others can be safe and reliable? If so, with whom (this can be a pet)?

   ____

   ____

   ____

2. If I've felt securely attached to someone, what sorts of thoughts or feelings do I have with this person or animal? If I haven't experienced this yet, what sorts of thoughts or feelings do I imagine I'd have when I feel safe with someone?

3. Do I know anyone with a secure attachment style? How would I describe them? How do they show up in their relationships? How do they take care of themselves?

4. What is my greatest wish from a place of secure attachment?

5. What are ways I block this wish? Just notice this.

6. Is there anything I can identify to help build my secure part?

Example as Lara

1. Yes, I feel safe with my cousin and best friend.
2. It's just "easy" around them.
3. My cousin definitely seems securely attached. She's good at setting boundaries and taking care of herself without feeling selfish. She takes good care of herself mentally and physically.
4. My securely attached wish is for it to feel easier planning to have a family with Josue.
5. Instead of directly communicating, which would be easier in the long run, I drop hints most of the time with Josue.
6. I can open up to him about my insecurities about how he doesn't want kids with me without being blaming.

Example as Josue

1. I feel securely attached with my mom.
2. I feel like I can tell her anything and it'd be okay.
3. No, I don't. All my friends have relationship issues.
4. My greatest wish is that I could be a good dad and have kids with Lara.
5. I fixate on how my dad was "bad" to me and am constantly on the lookout for signs of this in me. When I feel angry, I'm really scared.
6. I can tell Lara I do want to have kids but my relationship with my dad makes me nervous. Maybe she could understand this?

EXERCISE: Coming Home to Safety

Understanding what safety—and a lack of it—literally *feels* like for you is a crucial part of building your secure attachment. In this exercise, you'll build this awareness. Moving forward, this helps you know when you feel safe or in danger. Once you are aware of your feelings, you may take a step back to assess whether you are in attunement with the threat in order to make securely attached choices.

1. When you feel unsafe with someone (whether this is in attunement or not to the danger presented) how do you feel? Think about the emotions and physical sensations that may arise, such as panic in your chest or the desire to run away. It could also be the feeling of wanting to cling and obsess as other examples.

____

____

____

____

____

2. Describe what safety feels like or what you imagine it feels like. Common examples include warmth and coziness. If there is anyone you identified whom you feel safe with in the last exercise, contemplate how you feel around them both emotionally and physically.

____

____

____

____

____

3. In the box below, draw a place where you can feel truly safe. This could be from real life or just a safe place you imagine. Try to come up with as many details as possible. What would you see here? What would it smell or sound like? Try to consider the details you could draw to represent this, like a vanilla-scented candle or a trickling water feature. What would the weather be like if it's outdoors? Let yourself be as creative as possible. Please try to accept your drawing as is—you're doing this to help you feel safer rather than cultivating art skills.

4. Were you alone in your drawing? Or were other people in your safe place? Contemplate what your drawing tells you about your sense of safety in regard to others. Are there any other things you can identify about how you can feel safer from your picture?

____

____

____

Great job! You are now invited to bring in more of what already makes you feel safe to build your secure attachment. You will also learn how to set boundaries around the things that make you feel unsafe later on. But for now, focus on feeling literally safer, and you're well on your way to recovery!

Becoming Securely Attached Chapter Reminders

You've done a wonderful job in this chapter of planting seeds to become more securely attached. This is how you truly recover from toxic relationship patterns, rather than fighting your nonsecure parts *or* just finding a new partner. Your happy, healthy relationship starts with changing your relationship with yourself.

- Close relationships are necessary for a happy, healthy life.
- Without close connections, your mental and physical health suffers.
- Nonsecure attachment confuses what is safe and unsafe, leading you to perhaps not protect yourself when you're in danger and/or making you flee from healthy intimacy.
- Learning to act as if you're securely attached is the key to growing this part.
- Becoming kinder toward yourself and working to judge yourself less harshly helps you become safer for yourself (and others).
- It's okay if you don't feel comfortable with the idea of self-love—all you need is an open mind throughout this process.
- Cultivating the practices and relationships in which you can feel safe helps grow your secure base.

Chapter 5

UNDERSTANDING YOUR NONSECURE ATTACHMENT

At this point, you may question *why* you struggle to feel safe with others even when they pose no threat, or you cling to people who are unsafe. This cannot be explored without acknowledging the impact of past painful situations. All human beings have experienced situations or events that deeply hurt, leaving lasting scars. These painful events are called "trauma," which stems from the Greek word for "wound." Trauma impacts your ability to connect and feel safe with yourself and others. There are a range of traumatic experiences in life that impact safety, including natural disasters. However, when discussing attachment, it is the wounding that happens in relationships that is typically the most damaging.

When a person thinks about their trauma, they may have a wide range of intense emotions. If you relate, please take breaks as needed while being compassionate and self-validating. These emotions are understandable. In chapter 6, you'll learn more tools to help soothe you. If possible, you may also benefit from working with a trauma therapist for personalized support. The Resources section gives tools for finding a therapist and other support for trauma healing.

Other times, a person experiences strong feelings when they hear about "trauma" because they believe they did not experience any. A common reaction here is to feel protective of your parents. This is understandable, and there are many types of trauma, in both adulthood and childhood, that can lead to nonsecure attachment. Additionally, some attachment wounds may be harder to identify than others.

Trauma Stemming from Abuse and Neglect

The wounds that are typically most obvious involve abuse and neglect. These understandably can lead to a nonsecure attachment style. Just as in romantic relationships, abuse can take many forms in childhood, such as physical, sexual, or psychological. The people who inflict this abuse may be family, foster parents, teachers, coaches, and religious leaders, to give some examples. Abuse, as it's inherently violating to one's body and/or mind, damages a person's ability to feel safe, believe in their worth, and trust themselves or others. Through this lens, it is natural to have compassion for someone's anxious or avoidant parts.

Neglect can also create a nonsecure attachment style. Regardless of a parent's intentions, neglect often leads a child to feel unworthy and unsafe. Neglect may happen as a complete absence of caring for a child's physical needs, such as not having reliable food. Other times, a neglectful parent is literally absent or emotionally unavailable. A less obvious wound of neglect involves having your material needs cared for but having a lack of warmth in your home. This includes never being hugged or told "I love you" growing up.

A lack of guidance from your parents may also create a wound of neglect. A person may have had their needs met growing up, but if a parent doesn't teach them how to be self-sufficient, such as how to cook for themselves or care for their body, this neglect may make them overly insecure or dependent on others. Finally, a lack of healthy rules and limits is neglectful. This child naturally doesn't learn how to appropriately engage with others. Not having consequences, for instance, makes a child feel unsafe (as they don't know what to expect) *and* makes them less likely to consider how they impact others. This, of course, makes it difficult to form secure bonds.

Trauma Stemming from Enmeshment

A commonly overlooked trauma is *too much closeness* with someone growing up, which is often referred to as "enmeshment." For example, when a parent wants their child to be their best friend, or a surrogate parent or partner, this negatively impacts their child's ability to be securely attached. Or this can happen when parents expect a child to perform athletically and/or academically to make their family look good. This is too much closeness because the parents are extracting a sense of self from the child. In these roles of being a great student or best friend, a child may feel special, and yet still be harmed. These roles lead the child to believe that to be accepted in relationships, they are obligated to sacrifice for others' happiness. They may also only feel worthy when others need them, or they are achieving. This limits their ability to experience relationships as a safe place to be authentic.

Another example of how too much closeness can be damaging (which is also psychological abuse) is consistently being told what you "should" think, feel, or believe. This sends the message to the child that their belonging is conditional, which creates nonsecure attachment. On the other hand, when a person has secure attachment, they learn that they belong simply because they exist within their family or among their peers. There's a natural sense of trust, safety, and ability to give *and* receive support.

Other Influences on Nonsecure Attachment Styles

There are other painful experiences outside of your family dynamic that can contribute to a nonsecure attachment style. For instance, if you were bullied growing up or had to move a lot and never had lasting friends, these may impact your ability to attach securely to others. A person may cope with these experiences by learning to hide their authentic self to "fit in," which may lead to anxious attachment. Or they may cope with this pain by disengaging socially to protect themselves, which can lead to avoidance.

Other very wounding events include the larger community you lived within being harsh, rejecting, or violent. For example, if you experienced systemic discrimination such as homophobia, racism, ableism, or classism (judgment from others for being in poverty, for instance), you may also struggle to feel safe, worthy, and/or trust others. As clinician Deb Dana explains, "Trauma compromises our ability to engage with others by replacing patterns of connection with patterns of protection" (2018).

Secure Attachment Can Be Wounded

Other times, a person grows up feeling safe, trusting, and confident in their relationships, yet sadly, their secure attachment is damaged in adulthood. The trauma of being cheated on by a close partner, for instance, may lead you to become anxious and/or avoidant in later relationships. Being scammed, manipulated, or abused by a friend, romantic partner, or someone you met online may also damage your attachment style. Abuse that occurs outside of childhood can naturally impact a person's attachment style as well.

Furthermore, while a person with a secure attachment style will typically set boundaries on abuse or mistreatment because they trust in their worth, a lot of abuse can be covert or even completely absent until a person seriously commits. For instance, numerous clients I have worked with felt their relationship was "perfect" or "amazing" until they got married. It was only when they married that their partner became controlling or abusive. Sadly, for some, this switch even happened on their honeymoon. Of course, once a person has committed, it's harder to leave a relationship. Over time, the abuse can make them develop nonsecure attachment. And sadly, an abusive partner often exploits the person's reactions to the abuse as "crazy," further reinforcing toxic and abusive cycles that continue to degrade the person's sense of worth and options.

Finally, toxic relationships often are inherently traumatic. This is true even if you aren't aware of the lasting scars your toxic relationship has left. For instance, even as a trauma therapist, I didn't realize my last toxic relationship was actually traumatic until *years later.* This awareness happened when I saw his number pop up on the phone and I began to shake, cry, and dissociate (the feeling of leaving your body).

While you may have only experienced your attachment injuries as an adult, for many people with a toxic relationship history, they've experienced complex wounding in both childhood and adulthood. Wherever you find yourself right now, please know you are not bad, broken, or hopeless. As Peter Levine, one of the world's leading trauma experts, explains, "Trauma is a fact of life. It does not, however, need to be a life sentence. Not only can trauma be healed, but with appropriate guidance and support, it can be transformative" (Levine and Frederick 1997).

The Ripple Effect of Trauma

Right now, you may notice different emotions arising. You may feel protective of your family. Or you may feel anger or resentment. Pain and shame are also common reactions to discussing trauma. Whatever you feel, please know there is no problem with it. You are allowed to feel any and all emotions, as these are a part of being human and none are "bad" or "wrong." Of course, what you do with your emotions can help or add suffering, but learning to be a safe person for yourself involves accepting your emotions.

Whatever you feel, it may be helpful to acknowledge that most parents are trying their best *and* children may still get wounded. Unless, and until, a person does their own healing work, it's human nature to replicate—or react to—our own wounds. Your parents (or whoever harmed you) were likely acting out of their wounds. Yet of course, this does not make it okay that they hurt you.

You *never* deserved to be harmed, neglected, abused, or mistreated. Your trauma is not a reflection of your worth—or the nature of all human beings. You are innately whole and valuable. Rather, these wounds simply mean you were around unhealed people acting out of their own pain.

Your trauma is an unfortunate, regrettable part of your life's journey. But your past does not dictate your future. You are absolutely capable of healing. Moving forward, your life can be filled with the joy of authentic confidence, true belonging, and intimacy.

• CASE STUDY: *Kyle*

Kyle's father died when he was just a baby. His mom never remarried and focused all her attention on him. She often told him how handsome, smart, and funny he was. She never put pressure on him about school because she hated how her parents had pressured her. Instead, she wanted him to enjoy his childhood and catered to his every want. Kyle grew up feeling loved, but never learned how to take care of himself. As a result, when he went to college, he immediately got a girlfriend, Rochelle, who helps do his homework and does his laundry. Sometimes, Kyle cheats on her at parties because he's not quite sure he likes her that much. But he's afraid he can't take care of himself.

EXERCISE: Honoring Your Wounds

In this exercise, you will begin to explore how your attachment was wounded. You'll do this by honoring one memory that feels connected to your anxious and/or avoidant attachment. You can pick the earliest memory that stands out, a collection of memories such as being bullied, or anything that feels right for now. If many memories come up, please just pick one that's manageable to look at for now. It's not kind to excavate all your trauma all at once—and you may need the support of a therapist to dive deeper. You don't need to put pressure on yourself. You will recover in your own right time—and it's healthy to take breaks as you need. When looking at your wounds, please remember that no one has to be "wrong" or "bad." Rather, you are simply acknowledging how your nonsecure attachment *is* understandable, which reduces confusion and self-judgment. If you don't relate to the idea of having trauma, try to identify a memory from the past that you wish hadn't happened and perhaps leaves a bitter or sour feeling.

You will consider how this memory or experience impacted your view about yourself *and* others. Finally, as your core whole Self, acting as a securely attached parent, you'll affirm your nonsecure part to transform negative beliefs. This affirmation allows you to reframe any negative beliefs while encouraging yourself like a loving parent would if you felt insecure or uncertain. Please see the written example for clarity as needed.

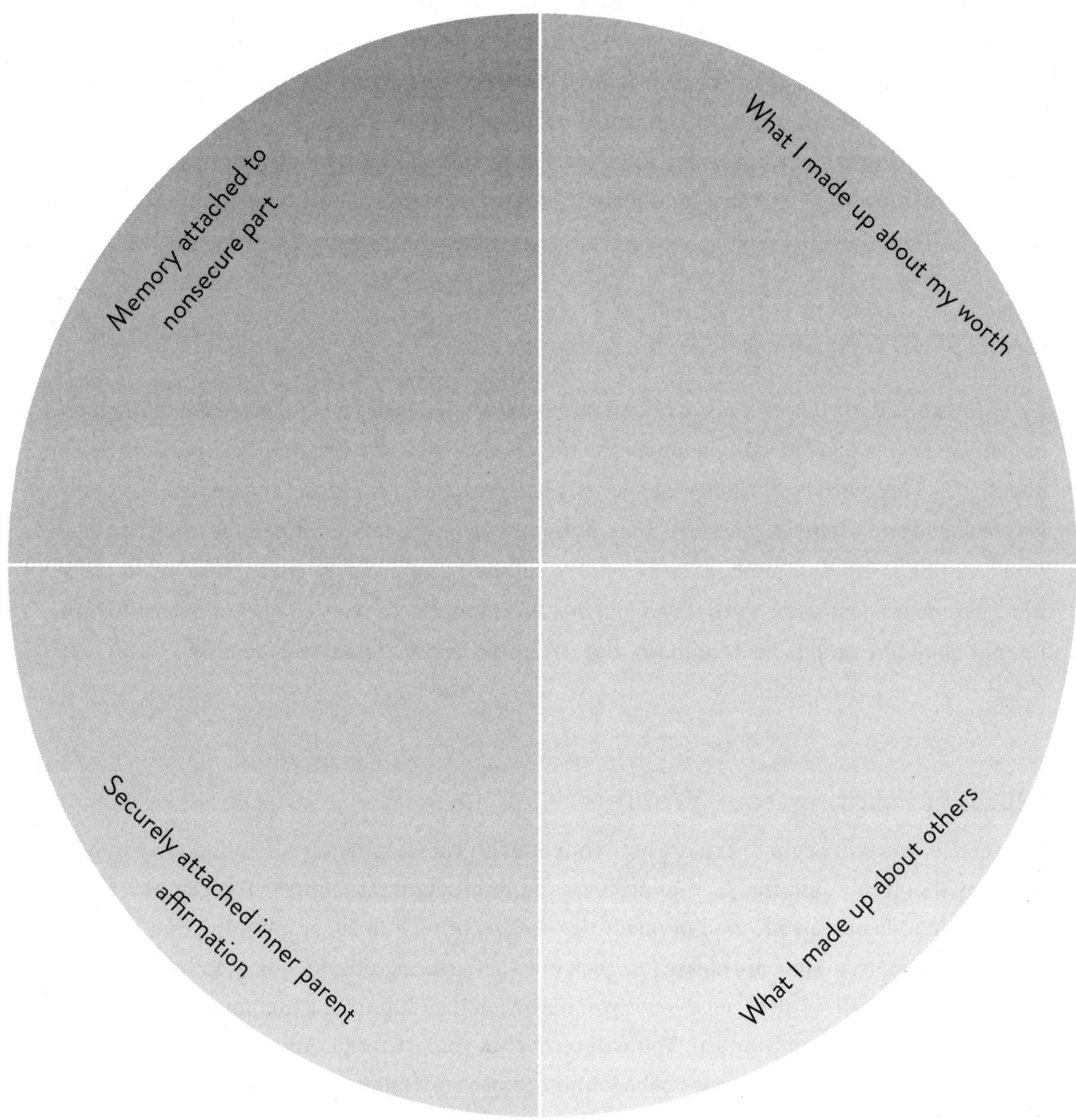
Memory attached to
nonsecure part
What I made up about my worth
Securely attached inner parent
affirmation
What I made up about others

EXAMPLE AS KYLE

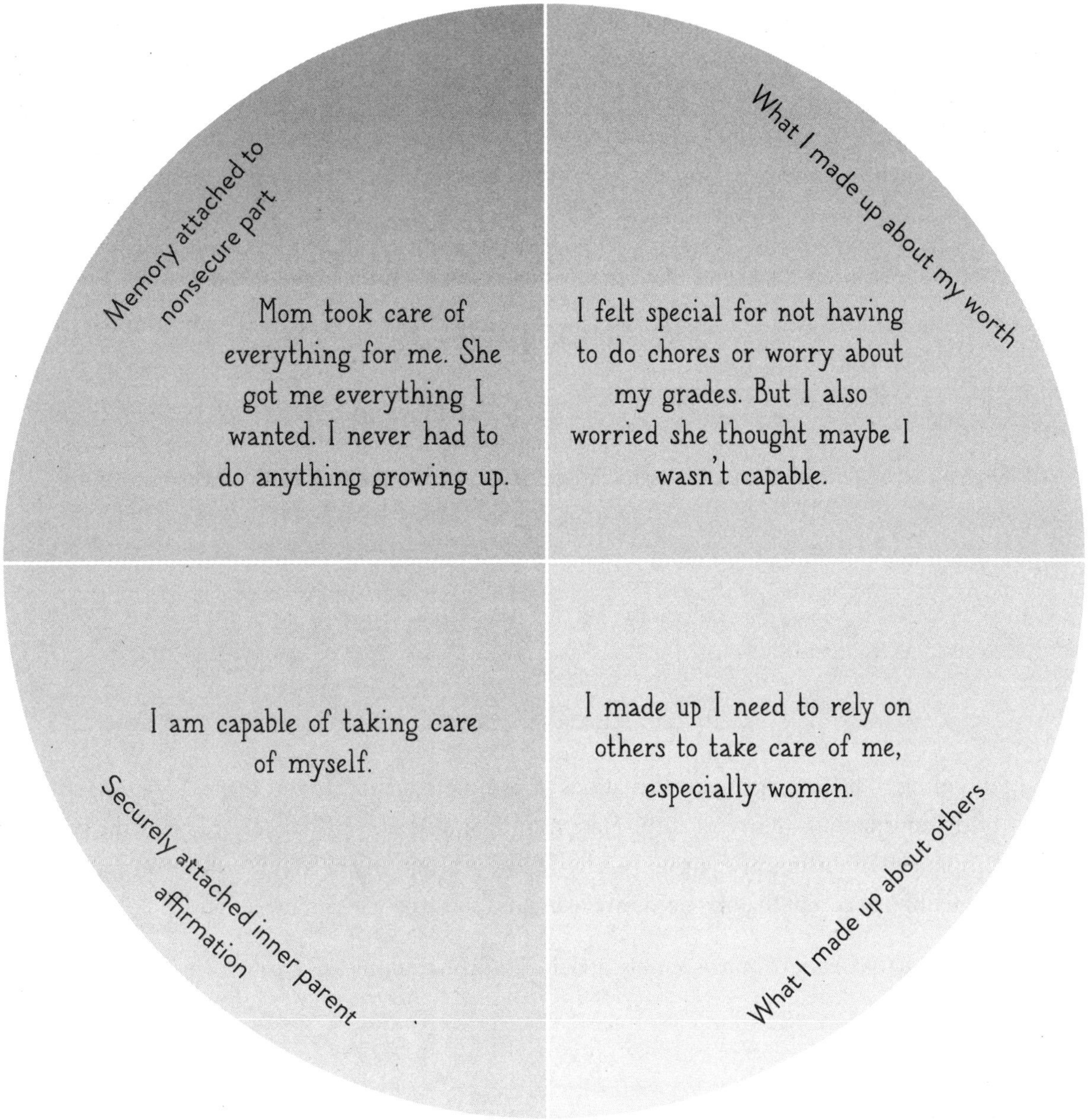

Memory attached to nonsecure part

Mom took care of everything for me. She got me everything I wanted. I never had to do anything growing up.

What I made up about my worth

I felt special for not having to do chores or worry about my grades. But I also worried she thought maybe I wasn't capable.

Securely attached inner parent affirmation

I am capable of taking care of myself.

What I made up about others

I made up I need to rely on others to take care of me, especially women.

Great job honoring your attachment wounds. Hopefully, you have a little more understanding and compassion for your past actions based on this.

EXERCISE: Affirming Your Parts as a Securely Attached Inner Parent

In the previous exercise, you created an affirmation as your securely attached parent. However, it's completely okay if you found this process a bit challenging. Toxic relationships, nonsecure attachment, and its underlying views often hurt your ability to feel connected to your whole, authentic Self and inherent, unconditional worth. Wherever you find yourself, it's natural if you struggle with affirming yourself right now or you find it cheesy. Just being willing to cultivate this practice, which you do here, supports your recovery.

1. Write your securely attached inner parent affirmation from the previous exercise:

   ____

   ____

2. Do you struggle to believe this affirmation? If so, what insecurities or uncertainties arise here?

   ____

   ____

   ____

3. Struggling to believe positive affirmations is common at first. If you relate, try creating a "bridge affirmation" (Mazzola 2019). Here you affirm you are working toward believing your affirmation. For instance, if you don't fully believe yet that "My needs are okay," you may say, "I'm willing to accept that my needs are okay, and some people can meet them."

   If you don't yet believe your securely attached affirmation, please create a "bridge affirmation" here:

   ____

   ____

   ____

   ____

4. Great! Now, bring your workbook to a mirror in a private space like your bathroom.

5. Pause to look at yourself in the mirror. If you find this is too overwhelming, try looking only into your eyes rather than at your whole self. Now, say your affirmation aloud. Notice any feelings or physical sensations that arise. If you feel uncomfortable, try to breathe through it, remembering healing is sometimes uncomfortable as we are learning to do new things. You're doing a great job!

6. Please practice looking at yourself (or into your eyes), saying your (bridge) affirmation ten times aloud. It's okay to feel uncomfortable or silly. Recovering sometimes pushes you out of what's familiar, and that's a good thing.

7. Great job! What thoughts, feelings, or sensations arose during this activity?

____

____

____

____

____

Moving forward, try repeating your affirmation multiple times while looking at yourself at least once a day. You're helping yourself hear new, more positive, supportive thoughts when you may be in the habit of hearing more self-critical ones. This is tremendous recovery work!

Example as Kyle

1. I am capable of taking care of myself.

2. I don't really believe this. I don't know how to do laundry or even make eggs. I feel like a baby.

3. I can learn how to take care of myself.

7. It feels awkward but also like I really can learn how to make eggs, do laundry, and other chores.

Moving from Criticism to Compassion

You may have some harsh judgments about yourself or others, which you explored in the last chapter. These judgments stem from the beliefs you hold about yourself and others, which emerged from your wounds. These beliefs can reinforce toxic relationship patterns. For instance, if you believe "all women lie," the way you approach relationships is very different than someone who understands *some women* lie while others are trustworthy. Or if you think "I must be perfect," you'll naturally hide your insecurities and exhaust yourself performing for others. This, of course, keeps a close intimate relationship at bay, reinforcing the idea that you can't be yourself. These judgments are of course limiting, but it's important to be compassionate that they are a result of trauma.

To overcome these patterns of thinking from your wounding, practicing self-compassion is very helpful. This is an invaluable practice for securely attached relationships because the compassion—or loving, understanding warmth—that you withhold from yourself, you ultimately will withhold from others. And vice versa. The quality of your relationships is always dependent on the quality of the relationship you have with yourself. Research proves people who are self-compassionate have healthier, happier, and more connected relationships. Their partners view them as more accepting of their differences and more willing to communicate through concerns. Their partners also feel free to be their authentic, separate, unique self. These are stark differences between the controlling, suffocating, withdrawn, isolating, and miserable qualities often associated with toxic relationships.

Becoming more self-compassionate (and other-compassionate) is a practice that involves these core tenets (Neff, 2011):

- Mindfulness, which is simply full attention to the present moment without judging it
- Practicing kindness toward yourself, which includes interrupting self-critical thoughts with your securely attached affirmation
- Accepting your common humanity, which includes accepting that you and all others are equal human beings who will experience joy, pain, rejection, loss, and rewards *simply because you are alive* and not because anyone is better or less than anyone else

You've already begun this practice of being more self-compassionate and will continue to do so throughout this workbook. Cultivating self-compassion tremendously opens up your options to act securely attached.

EXERCISE: Mindfulness Scavenger Hunt

Depending on your wounds, you may struggle to be kind to yourself and/or others. This is completely okay and understandable. By practicing mindfulness, a more balanced view of yourself and others will eventually come naturally. This is where secure attachment lies. In this activity, you will practice becoming more mindful.

1. Move around your current space and find five objects that feel smooth to touch, like a glass object. Try to fully immerse yourself in this activity without judging it. You're not "wasting time" and there's a point. Try to approach this like a child on a scavenger hunt. Write down these five items here:

   ____

   ____

   ____

   ____

   ____

2. Now repeat this to find six objects that are yellow. Write down what you find here:

   ____

   ____

   ____

   ____

   ____

   ____

3. Next find three words in your space (or you can scan this workbook) that inspire you. Write them down here:

____

____

____

Awesome job! You just practiced mindfulness by fully engaging with this activity without judging it. When you act as if whatever you're doing right now, like finding a word, is the only thing that matters, you are mindful. This practice naturally interrupts patterns of thinking critically about yourself, others, or the world. It truly can be this simple to cultivate more compassion and peace!

Waiting to Be Rescued

Our wounds can lead many of us to mistakenly believe that one day someone will save us from feeling worthless, scared, uncertain, or powerless ever again. This is why when someone you're dating makes a mistake, you can be so hard on them. Or you can be so willing to ignore blatant red flags. You just want to be saved by some perfect, all-understanding and all-loving person. This fantasy is often reinforced by our culture as well. But it's just that—a fantasy.

The illusion that someone can save you from human experiences like insecurity or loss isn't true. And this fantasy perpetuates toxic relationships. Firstly, it's inherently disempowering, which reinforces clinging to unhealthy relationships. You are already whole and equally worthy to all others as your core Self. Furthermore, when we date from this place, we often are attracted to the very people who will most likely trigger our past wounds, such as a workaholic like dad or someone who's emotionally volatile like mom. Or we date people "completely opposite" to the people who first hurt us, but are inevitably crushed when they're imperfect.

To escape this dynamic, you must accept that no one else can "rescue" you or make you worthy. You already are worthy! Furthermore, as your whole, compassionate, and accepting Self, you are the person best equipped to care for yourself.

EXERCISE: Being Your Own Rescuer

In this activity, you will imagine rescuing yourself from a past hurtful situation with another person. This may feel odd at first, and that's okay. An open mind and commitment to yourself are your best assets as you recover! Finally, there is no "perfect" in this process, just what feels right to you.

1. Identify a painful memory from at least five years ago that involved another person. Try to pick a situation you wish hadn't happened but one you can tolerate looking at for a period of time. If a situation that feels too bad comes up, try putting it in an imaginary box for you to revisit when it feels more tolerable. Write down what happened here:

   ____

   ____

   ____

   ____

   ____

   ____

   ____

2. Imagine going back in time to find your past self. Go to the place you will find this version of yourself—this could be where the memory happened or just where you associate with this past version of yourself, like an old bedroom. You are here to listen without judgment to this part that's hurting. If someone you felt safe with expressed a genuine interest in what you were thinking and feeling at this time, what would you have said back then?

   ____

   ____

   ____

3. As your whole Self embodying a securely attached parent, write out what understanding you can provide to this past self. Why do their feelings and thoughts make sense? Try to really validate them before rushing to "make it okay." A lot of times, the parts of us that still hurt just need to be listened to first.

4. Now provide insight into what you now know about this situation or your worth. You may want to reassure yourself that you will survive this pain, as your current self is proof of that. Write out any newer perspectives you have here:

5. You don't have to leave this part of you in the past anymore where it's hurting and lonely. In your imagination, explore if this part of you is willing to come to the present day with you. If yes, please go to step 6. If not, what else does this part need from you to feel safe enough to come into the present and leave this past behind?

6. Imagine this part of you develops wings and can fly away from this past pain. Let this part fly to greet you in the present day where you are now and imagine them integrating into your body wherever it feels right to do this, like your heart or your shoulder. Write down anything you notice here:

____

____

____

7. Draw a picture of what it feels like or looks like in your mind's eye to be more whole again once you've rescued this part of you from the past. You can't go wrong with whatever you want to draw; just allow yourself to tap into this sense of being more whole. If you prefer, though, feel free to write a word, sentence, or phrase that comes to mind here instead.

Example as Kyle

1. Growing up, it felt like I couldn't ask questions about my dad because my mom would get so sad. I felt sad, confused, lonely, and angry.
2. I'm in my backyard—I'd say, "I'm sad I don't have a dad to play basketball with this ball I got for my birthday."
3. I'd say to my past self, "It makes sense you feel sad. It feels weird being angry at dad for dying, but it's okay to be mad. You were robbed! Mom's great, but she's not a guy. She can't teach you things about being a boy like your dad could've."
4. Well, we learned how to survive, obviously, but I guess that pain still lives inside of me. I'm realizing I have to let myself feel sad about not having a dad instead of burying it.
5. He wants me to promise to play basketball with him. I'll do that.
6. It feels lighter and calmer.
7. "We can play basketball together, younger me."

Wonderful job caring for a part of you that was hurt in the past. While you can't change what happened back then, you can show up for yourself as a safe, consistent, and reliable person. This builds your secure attachment while making your overall life more peaceful and joyful.

Understanding Your Nonsecure Attachment Chapter Reminders

- All human beings have experienced wounding events known as trauma—and it's these wounds that have impacted your sense of authentic belonging and safety with others, leading to nonsecure attachment.

- You can absolutely heal from trauma, which includes learning how to show up for yourself compassionately and mindfully.

- Every time you interrupt harsh, judgmental thoughts by practicing mindfulness, you are healing.

- You are already whole and the person best equipped to take care of yourself through life's natural ups and downs, which includes other people—even safe people—disappointing you in the future.

Chapter 6

BECOMING WHOLE: COMING BACK HOME TO YOURSELF

In the last chapter, you honored your wounds, which often impact your ability to feel safe connecting with others authentically. These wounds, while they're not your fault, often make you feel "broken" or "damaged" in some way. In this chapter, you will begin to reclaim a sense of wholeness. While you have understandably engaged in relationships in a nonsecure way, you have never been inherently damaged or broken. You will deepen the work you've begun to cultivate a secure attachment style *within* yourself, *for* yourself. When you have a fully safe home within yourself, you are able to tolerate intimacy, rejection, and conflict with maturity and wisdom. To feel safe and whole, you must learn to fully and unconditionally support one of the most basic parts of your humanity—your emotions.

Unfortunately, for many, the ability to *feel* emotions—let alone cope with them in a lovingly accepting way—is often denied. Upon discovering that this chapter focuses on emotions, you may have felt uncomfortable. Common thoughts here are "this is a waste of time," or "emotions are just an inconvenience," or "I don't want to do this." If you had a similar thought, this is completely okay. It's understandable to feel uncomfortable about your emotions, and yet, denying your emotions may contribute to toxic relationship cycles.

Consider how often an imbalanced approach to feeling your emotions, whether it was overexpressing them or ignoring them, contributed to your toxic relationship. Maybe you suppressed anger toward your ex but found yourself suddenly launching into a tirade of criticisms when you "couldn't handle it any longer." Then you may have found yourself feeling ashamed *and* your valid concerns were swept under the rug because you were the one who "acted poorly." This common example highlights how ignoring emotions poses more damage to yourself and relationships than embracing them wisely. Now, you are learning to support your whole Self, which includes unconditionally accepting and nurturing your emotions.

EXERCISE: Being Present

Your emotions, even if they are about the past or the future, live in the now. You can only *feel* things in the present moment. Connecting to your emotions mindfully is the first step to coping well. You must first know you are feeling something intensely to care for yourself appropriately.

In this activity, you will practice being present.

1. To be truly mindful, please eliminate distractions. Move to a quiet spot where you can be alone, without any device tempting you to check it. If you can go outside where you feel safe, such as your back patio, this is even better.

2. Take a few breaths to settle down. In this exercise, you cannot do anything "right" or "wrong." Rather, you are practicing mindfulness, which is full attention to the moment without judging it as "good" or "bad."

3. Notice the sensations of the environment on your skin. This includes the warmth of the sun, a fan, or a cool breeze. Continue to breathe, simply noticing what you feel on your skin in as much detail as possible.

4. Great job. Now, soften your gaze to attune your ears to the sounds around you. There are no "good" or "bad" sounds when you are practicing mindfulness. Listen to the sounds around you while letting go of stories you may have, such as judging your neighbors if you hear a dog barking. If you're unable to hear your environment, sense for the vibrations of sound around you.

5. Take another breath and notice the qualities of light around you, like the moon reflecting off water or shade under trees. Try to be aware of all the different ways light reflects around you. Become aware of what happens to you physically, going through these prompts. Perhaps your body tightens, as an example.

6. Now simply notice what sensations you feel in your body. There are no right or wrong sensations, but some may be comfortable and others uncomfortable. Your mindfulness practice asks you to try accepting all sensations with an open mind. After taking some time, circle any sensations you felt (and add any you felt not listed here):

tense	tight	open	quiet
calm	light	heavy	achy
numb	tingly	soft	hard

7. Wonderful job getting in touch with yourself! What was this activity like for you physically? What emotions, if any, did you feel? Did you notice any thoughts arise, including those of judgments? (If you think, "I feel" but add "like" or "that," this is a thought, not an emotion; i.e., "I feel sad" is an emotion, whereas "I feel like I didn't do this right" is a thought. If so, please have compassion—judging is human, and it takes a lot of practice to not lean into judgment.)

____

____

____

You are building secure attachment as you practice mindful awareness of your experiences. This is important for healthy coping, as well as good communication. After all, you cannot intimately and kindly share with others about your experience if you're not aware of it.

To best support yourself in being securely attached from within and with others, you may choose to repeat this exercise daily—especially if you are often "numb" and/or stuck in obsessive thoughts about your ex or past.

Accepting Your Emotions

To be safe with yourself, you must cope with your emotions in healthy ways. Whether you are anxious, avoidant, or both, you likely have ways of reacting to emotions that are ultimately unhelpful. This includes coping strategies that may leave you feeling worse, such as hungover or ashamed. This also includes judgments around "unacceptable" emotions, which will naturally make you see yourself and/or others as the problem when these emotions are felt or expressed.

To become securely attached, you must accept your emotions as a part of being alive. Truly, there are no "bad" emotions—just comfortable and uncomfortable ones. Accepting your common humanity is part of being self-compassionate, which includes accepting that all emotions are human. Psychologist Susan David poignantly explains, "Only dead people never get unwanted or inconvenienced by their feelings. Only dead people never get stressed, never get broken hearts, never experience the disappointment that comes with failure. Tough emotions are part of our contract with life. You don't get to have a meaningful career, or raise a family, or leave the world a better place without stress or discomfort. Discomfort is the price of admission to a meaningful life" (2017).

• CASE STUDY: *Jack and Micah*

Jack and Micah hooked up the night they met. Jack was just looking for fun after his divorce, and initially, Micah thought that sounded good. However, it's been two years now of a "situationship," and Micah is increasingly anxious about becoming an official couple. Jack reminds Micah he never wanted this, but sends mixed messages, like telling Micah he's never felt so connected to anyone and he loves him. At the same time, Jack will brag about dating other people and describe his encounters to Micah. Thinking he just needs to be patient, Micah suppresses his feelings, but when he gets drunk, he'll sometimes yell and cry about how it's "not fair" and he knows Jack wants more. In the morning, Micah apologizes for being embarrassing and they sweep it under the rug, continuing the situationship.

EXERCISE: Your Relationship with Emotions

Feelings alone are never a problem. It's only our reactions, including our judgments about emotions, that can create problems. Please remember, your judgments are understandable and come from a place of survival. At the same time, becoming aware of personal attitudes about emotions, which may reinforce anxious and/or avoidant attachment, highlights new recovered ways of considering emotions.

In this exercise, you'll explore your judgments about emotions. In the columns below, please note automatic reactions related to the emotions listed. Try not to censor yourself. Your gut reaction, rather than what seems logically "right," is what we are interested in here. Examples of emotions for the columns (which you can add to) are:

- Disappointment
- Resentment
- Sadness, Despair, Hopelessness
- Anger, Irritation, Annoyance
- Love or Compassion
- Empathy or Forgiveness
- Sensitive, Vulnerable
- Lonely
- Fear, Anxiety, Nervousness, Scared
- Joy, Happiness
- Excitement, Hope
- Creative, Passionate, Inspired
- Sexual, Lustful
- Ashamed, Shame, Embarrassed
- Guilt, Regret

Emotions I should feel	Emotions I shouldn't feel

Whatever you wrote in each column, great job building awareness—this helps you recover!

Now, for the list of emotions you believe aren't acceptable to feel, such as anger, sadness, or fear, complete the following prompts. Repeat as needed for each emotion a part of you thinks you shouldn't feel.

1. The emotion I judge is:

____

____

2. When I consciously feel this way, I think and/or act in these ways:

____

____

____

____

3. When other people feel this emotion, I think:

____

____

____

____

4. My parents (or the people who raised me) expressed this emotion in the following ways:

____

____

____

____

____

5. When I felt this way growing up, they explicitly told me:

6. The message I picked up about this emotion is:

7. My judgment around this emotion played out in my last toxic relationship in the following ways:

Example as Micah

1. I judge my loneliness.
2. I think it's embarrassing, so I push it away. I'll call up guys who like me just to have some company even if I don't like them.
3. I never hear anyone talking about being lonely. It makes me think no one else feels this way, reinforcing my embarrassment.
4. My parents were always working. I'm not sure they ever felt lonely.
5. I never told them I felt lonely growing up.
6. They praised me for being such a "quiet, good boy." I learned that people like me better when I don't make waves.
7. I never tell Jack directly how I feel because I'm so embarrassed—and I know deep down, he doesn't want a commitment and I'm afraid I'll never feel this connected to someone again.

Reclaiming the Emotions You Judge

Internal Family Systems (IFS), as previously mentioned, is an attachment therapy founded on the idea that we all have different parts of self. When these are in disharmony, it creates inner conflict, suffering, and relationship problems. Healing invites you to become whole again as your Self. This Self acts like a securely attached parent in practice, bringing into conscious harmony all your parts, supporting them as needed. This internal harmony allows you to stop perpetuating cycles that harm yourself or others. To do this, you must reclaim parts of yourself you've previously rejected, your "exiles" (Schwartz 2023).

Exiles are the parts of you that were rejected or shamed by others. These are the parts that feel like they're "not enough," or alternatively, "too much" to be loved. There are two primary parts of us that get rejected by others, thus becoming exiled by ourselves to gain acceptance. These commonly exiled parts are:

1. Your sensitive parts, like your need for comfort such as physical touch and kind words as well as your emotions
2. Your authentically alive, joyful, creative, playful, and spontaneous parts

Your sensitive parts, like your emotions and need for connection, are commonly exiled when you pick up the message that these parts are a "burden" to others. Any time you were told directly, or indirectly, that emotions are weakness or unwelcome, leads to this exiling. Sometimes, you may have been mocked, called names, or told you would be "given a reason" to cry if you expressed your emotions. This is also true for having your needs mocked or neglected.

Your authentically alive parts can be exiled for many reasons, but common shaming messages that shut these parts down include being told often to "be quiet" or "tone it down." Or receiving hurtful, critical messages about your art or creative outlets, or being told they can't be a "real job." Never being given time to play and be spontaneous, such as growing up with rigid schedules, also exiles your aliveness.

These wounding experiences around our authentic aliveness (which does include our sensitivities!) make us reject these parts personally. The creator of IFS, Richard Schwartz, explains these parts become "toxic waste" to us, as we believe they make us less valuable. Yet, when we reclaim these parts, we see their "buried treasure" (2023). As your whole, vibrant Self, you see the beauty of your exiles. Your playfulness, for instance, adds so much joy to your life when you embrace it. From this wholesome place, you're no longer terrified of being fully seen, which is essential for healthy, secure intimacy.

EXERCISE: Connecting with an Exile

It can be difficult, at first, to identify your exiled parts. In this exercise, you will explore connecting with an exile. This process of becoming consciously acquainted with your exiles allows you to comfort these parts effectively when they feel triggered. Comforting your exiles helps you resolve any emptiness you may carry in time. Finally, internal wholeness helps you feel more emotionally stable. Please be patient with yourself during this activity. Sometimes, we've pushed an exile away so intensely, it takes time to recover it.

Please answer the following questions to locate an exile:

1. What thoughts, feelings, or beliefs arise when you think about being vulnerable? This includes being aware and actually *feeling* your emotions (as opposed to feeling numb or disconnected) and expressing these to other people, such as letting yourself cry and accepting support from others.

___

___

___

___

2. How do you feel about letting yourself do whatever sounds pleasant or fun at times and not having a "to-do" list or agenda? How do you feel about going with the flow and being spontaneous? Do you create space to be creative and playful at times? Do you ever find it difficult to relax?

3. Do you often feel drained? Or are you usually quite energized and expressive? Do you let yourself have authentic fun (as opposed to doing things that numb you, like drinking, overeating, or bingeing content)?

Your answers reveal where you may have an exile—or multiple ones.

4. Do you negatively judge vulnerability? If so, you likely have an exile around your emotions, needs, or sensitivity. When were these parts of you rejected or shamed? Consider how it makes sense that you may suppress your sensitive parts for a sense of belonging now.

5. Is your life very structured filled with "to-do" lists and routines? Do you avoid letting yourself do nothing at times? If so, this reveals your natural alive and spontaneous nature was likely exiled. Where do you think you picked up the message that it's not okay to do things just because they feel good, such as relaxing or having fun? Did you learn that your worth is connected to your accomplishments? Many people in Western culture pick up the message that they should always be productive rather than "lazy." Remember, these wounding messages may come from our larger culture rather than your family.

____

____

____

____

6. Do you feel drained and like something is sucking the life out of you? If so, you probably exiled your creativity and passions. Where were these parts of you rejected or shamed? Maybe you learned from a depressed parent that life is to be endured rather than enjoyed? Or that money is more important than joy in your work?

____

____

____

____

7. Do you notice any exiled parts? When recovering from toxic relationship dynamics, it's common to have multiple parts of you that were rejected, quieted, or shamed. List your exiles here.

- ______________________
- ______________________
- ______________________
- ______________________

Example as Micah

1. I never let people know what I need or feel because of how my parents reacted to my sister growing up. She would complain a lot about my parents being so busy. They would tell her to be more grateful for the roof over her head and food in her belly that their hard work provided. They would sometimes send her to her room if she cried about missing them. I learned that I need to be okay with whatever I get from others to not be rejected.
2. I never let myself relax and have a quiet night in—even when I want it. When I came out, I felt like I had to party to fit in. Now, I drink and go out even when I want to relax. I'm afraid if I'm not always down for a fun time, people will think I'm boring. My work sometimes suffers due to this.
3. Yes, I'm drained all the time. I'm either working or partying it seems. But I'm tired of partying. The most fun I ever had was acting in high school, but I became a lawyer to make my parents happy.
4. Yes, I judge my "negative" emotions like insecurity, loneliness, and neediness.
5. I'm busy all the time. I absolutely learned that my worth is connected to my income and career.
6. Yes, I hate my career—I wake up tired and drained by the idea of working before my day's even started.
7. I exiled my creative outlet of acting and writing scripts.

Amazing job! Reclaiming your exiled parts is tremendous progress toward becoming whole again!

EXERCISE: Securely Parenting the Exile

Once you become aware of your exiles, the next step is to show up as a securely attached parent who unconditionally accepts them. From this place, you know you have no bad parts. Here, you show yourself the unconditional love you've always deserved but perhaps didn't receive. At first, you may need to just practice acting and thinking in this way toward yourself before you *feel* it. That's okay—this is exactly what recovery work is all about!

1. Please choose one exile you identified in the previous exercise, such as your love for music (an exile related to aliveness) or your anger or jealousy (an exile related to your emotions). Write down this part here:

2. Now, write an understanding letter to this exile. You've been practicing self-validation and self-compassion, which you will continue here. In this letter, please express *why* you decided this part of you isn't okay. Then validate how this suppressed part may show up anyway in unhelpful ways, feeding toxic relationship patterns. Then consider what it would be like if you reclaimed this part. Express the possibility that what you learned about this part was false. Finally, commit to accepting this part of you with more love and attention, which you can do in baby steps.

Example as Micah

To my creativity and love of acting,

Growing up, I learned that you aren't "real." Your parents hated their work, but they made good money. They taught you that external success and validation are much more important than happiness! Now you have a successful job you hate but never express this to others. You feel like a failure professionally and personally with Jack—like you just can't get it together. And yet you're still there—my love of acting. Maybe you unconsciously create drama with Jack because you want to be expressed? I know my feelings are valid, but maybe not the way I act like I'm in a soap opera sometimes. Maybe if I allowed you to be expressed, like acting locally, I'd feel more whole, settled. I know I don't have to give up my career or Jack to do this. I commit to you that I will go research how to audition for a local company. I already feel better!

Love,

Me

Wonderful job! Even if you don't fully feel like a securely attached parent to yourself, you're doing tremendously important recovery work by practicing. This practice is the true seed of secure attachment and recovery.

Nonsecure Ways of Coping with Emotions

Many people with nonsecure attachment didn't have healthy role models growing up for coping well with emotions. Instead, you may have witnessed your parents or others cope with overwhelming emotions in unhelpful ways. Without the guidance of a securely attached adult to show us we are still valuable when we feel intense emotions *and* that there are healthy ways to process emotions, we can get stuck in unhealthy ways of coping too. Coping strategies that ultimately hurt us more than help us are incredibly common through numbing and avoidant behaviors, like addictive overconsumption of food, alcohol, drugs, or content.

Obsession is another common strategy to distance us from emotions. For avoidants, this obsession commonly occurs outside of the relationship, and may take the form of an addiction as well, such as with substance abuse or workaholism. Anxiously attached people often turn their object of desire (which includes an ex) into the obsession. They often feel a sort of addictive craving toward this person. It's also common for nonsecurely attached people to use others to distract themselves from uncomfortable emotions. We can *use* others to provide us attention, compliments, their vulnerability, and/or sex to *feel better* internally. Of course, this is short-lived, and when we use others, we may later feel guilty—while perhaps creating conflict with the other person, who will naturally have feelings about being used.

These understandable coping strategies often leave us feeling stuck in toxic patterns. The part of you that copes with overwhelming emotions through self-harm, dissociation, obsession, and compulsion is called the "firefighter" in IFS. Dissociation is the opposite of mindfulness. It is when you feel numb to the point of no longer being in your body. This happens to both anxiously and avoidantly attached people, but those who are avoidant more often say they feel empty or like robots. Novelist Nathan Hill perfectly captures this when describing a character's experience in the book *Wellness*: "How little of herself had she offered up to those who loved her most?… Maybe something was broken within her. Maybe she wasn't feeling what she should be feeling. Maybe she understood love not as an emotion but a theoretical construct…just a well-researched simulation of what real people felt when they felt love" (2023).

Coping with Your Emotions as Your Secure Self

It's understandable you may have firefighter parts trying to keep you safe, which ultimately react in harmful ways. Just as you aren't "fighting" your anxious and/or avoidant parts, you aren't going to battle with your firefighters. Rather, you grow the part of you that is learning to cope well with your emotions.

Please have compassion for ways you may disconnect or react unhelpfully to emotions as attempts to survive. And as you're recovering, you are now able to let go of the things that helped you survive to learn to truly thrive. The practice is to now cope with your emotions as if a securely attached parent is soothing them without judgment, shame, or unhelpful reactions.

Self-Soothing to Feel Safe with Yourself

To feel safe and at home with yourself, you must treat your emotions kindly. You do this whether you know "why" you feel a certain way. One of the biggest traps for therapy clients that I often see is the belief that they need to understand *why exactly* they feel a certain way in order to feel okay. But emotions need to be *felt* rather than intellectualized. Sometimes, you are able to validate when your emotion does *make sense* given the situation or your experiences. You've already practiced doing this, and please continue to whenever possible. Yet you won't always understand logically where an emotion is coming from. Many people, maybe yourself included, have felt a sudden wave of sadness or anxiety with no known trigger. This is okay and you can still cope well with the emotion even if you don't know where it came from. Sometimes our emotions have roots in past traumas that are now making their way to the surface. For instance, if you weren't allowed to express anger growing up but are now recovering, you may feel intense anger in situations where it doesn't "make sense." This past anger coming up is resolved by *feeling and soothing it now.*

Other times, your emotion may arise because someone near you is feeling that way. A lot of people, especially those with an anxious attachment style, identify as sensitive or empathic. Empathy is a beautiful thing when paired with healthy confidence, boundaries, and coping skills. If you relate to having deep empathy, if you feel an intense emotion but don't know "why," try just caring for yourself rather than figuring it out or caretaking. Part of secure attachment involves prioritizing your care when you're dysregulated.

Finally, emotions are often complex and multilayered. Trying to figure them out may push you into a binary that's not realistic. For example, in a toxic relationship, your ex was likely the source of some of your greatest love and passion, and also the source of some of your greatest despair. All of these emotions are true, valid, and deserve care through healthy self-soothing. This is simply engaging in activities that calm your nervous system and provide relief without causing future issues. Your securely attached Self that you are cultivating throughout this workbook is a trustworthy guide to soothe yourself without self-betrayal. For instance, rather than calling someone who uses you when you feel lonely, your securely attached Self will guide you to do an inner child meditation. Or instead of getting drunk the night before a big interview, your securely attached Self will guide you to take a walk to cope with anxiety. You act as a parent reinforcing secure attachment with their child by being consistently reliable, trustworthy, and comforting.

EXERCISE: Self-Soothing Ideas

This list aims to inspire you to notice all the soothing activities available. Circle any you know you like. Also, please add in soothing activities you like that aren't on this list, like playing music. Finally, some of these options may sound strange, but the more open-minded you can be about trying them, the more readily you'll find what helps you and build your personal self-soothing tool kit. Underline any you're open to trying.

- Connect with your pet
- Paint your nails
- Do a face mask
- Watch ASMR
- Do a guided meditation
- Hug yourself

- Practice gentle yoga or stretching
- Take a nature walk
- Swim
- Visualize talking to your inner child to comfort them about the situation
- Look at the sky mindfully
- Practice deep breathing
- Wrap yourself in a warm blanket
- Journal a letter to the person you feel emotional toward to get out the feelings without needing to filter what you're saying (don't share this letter, but use it later to assess what boundaries you may need to set with them)
- Read about mindfulness or self-compassion
- Read a fun novel to feel some safe escape
- Wash dishes mindfully: feel the water on your hands and refocus your attention on this repeatedly
- Take a warm or cool shower or bath
- Use aromatherapy
- Drink some herbal tea
- Paint, draw, or do a craft
- ______________________________
- ______________________________
- ______________________________
- ______________________________
- ______________________________
- ______________________________

EXERCISE: Soothing Yourself with Compassion

In this exercise, you'll practice the fundamentals of soothing your distressing emotions, including anger, sadness, and self-loathing. The most important thing is to simply be willing to repeat this practice whenever you're dysregulated. Finally, you may not feel "better" right away when you self-soothe, but the goal is to at least prevent feeling worse by reacting to your emotions in unhelpful ways.

1. Connect with your emotions. Become aware of what you are feeling—both emotionally, if possible, and literally, as emotions are tied to physical sensations.

2. Whatever you feel, practice noticing the emotions and thoughts associated with it without judgment. Simply allow it to be. Say aloud, "I notice I feel" and insert your emotion or sensation. Or say, "I notice I have the thought that" and complete the sentence.

3. Practice accepting your thoughts, feelings, or sensations. Without making them "right" or "wrong," they will pass in a moment like clouds in the sky. You don't need to find a reason or someone to blame for these thoughts or feelings. You may practice validating yourself for extra comfort.

4. Now that you've accepted these feelings, you may comfort yourself from a mindful, compassionate place. Consider what will feel comforting right now. Notice you may have the automatic urge to do something that later makes you feel bad, like disconnecting on social media. See if you can find a replacement that actually is comforting, like taking some breaths, petting your dog, or taking a bath. Sometimes, just a distraction like doing dishes can also take the edge off intense feelings. Whatever feels "right" and comforting is correct for you. For ideas, look at the self-soothing list provided earlier.

5. Lean in and practice giving yourself this comfort that you have asked yourself for—if it's not the right time to do this, commit to doing this later and follow through like a loving parent. Maybe, for instance, you can't get a massage right now, but you can promise to give yourself a foot massage tonight with some coconut oil. Also, try something small in the interim like giving yourself a hug or looking at flowers outside.

6. Follow through on your commitments to yourself to build secure attachment from within.

Wonderful job—please repeat this practice as many times as needed, even if it feels like it's constant on some days. It may seem tedious, but it's better than the alternatives that perpetuate toxic cycles.

Example as Micah

1 and 2. I notice I feel sadness as pain in my chest over how I've lost myself.

3. It makes sense that I'm sad I've lost my creativity. It makes me feel most alive.

4. I'm going to let myself cry—I haven't let myself do that in a long time.

5 and 6. I couldn't cry much—it's been so long. But I feel a little tired in a good way now.

Becoming Whole: Coming Back Home to Yourself
Chapter Reminders

You've done a wonderful job reclaiming a sense of wholeness by unconditionally caring for your emotions in healthy ways. This is a tangible way you can consistently foster security and safety within yourself. Moving forward, please remember:

- Emotions are fundamental to being human.
- There are no "bad" or "wrong" emotions, only comfortable and uncomfortable ones.
- Judgments about emotions may reinforce nonsecure attachment and toxic relationship cycles.
- You may reclaim your natural emotions, sensitivity, aliveness, and creativity to be more whole.
- Ignoring, denying, going numb, or overexaggerating emotions are common reactions to discomfort, which reinforce toxic relationship cycles.
- Urges to react to emotions in ways that ultimately harm you or others are natural.
- You can cope well by first becoming mindful and then self-soothing.
- Coping well with your emotions allows you to feel safe and at home with yourself.

Chapter 7

GROUNDING INTO REALITY FOR SECURITY

In the last chapter, you began reclaiming a sense of wholeness to foster security within yourself no matter where you go or whom you interact with. You will now expand on this sense of grounded safety by exploring your relationship with reality. This is an essential skill before you cultivate healthy relationship skills in the next chapter. To be truly secure and safe within yourself and for another person, you must be grounded in actual reality.

The idea of having a "relationship with reality" may sound odd at first. This is completely understandable, as it's rare that this topic is overtly discussed. Your relationship with reality includes your beliefs, opinions, and perceptions and may sometimes be rooted in what you mindfully observe. Yet other times, your relationship with reality is based on the past rather than the present.

Your relationship with reality is reflected in the life you have today. When you explore where you are in life, you may work backward to clearly see your beliefs and perceptions that are working for you—as well as the ones that aren't. This is not to say that there aren't systemic issues impacting your current life, such as racism, sexism, or homophobia. Yet there are ways that your personal beliefs about yourself, others, and what's available to you have impacted your life—your toxic relationship history is a clear example of this. If you don't heal your relationship with reality, you will unfortunately recreate toxic relationship patterns in your future. This may be a fact you're sadly familiar with already.

Often, with nonsecure attachment and its related trauma, reality can be distorted. What you *know* to be true may become confused with your fears or insecurities. This cloudy relationship with reality includes the misattunement between accurately assessing safety and threats, as discussed previously. But there are other ways that confusion or numbness around reality may perpetuate toxic relationships. To recover, you must fully awaken to reality for what it mindfully is, rather than getting lost in projections based in fear, mistrust, or insecurity. Once you clearly see reality for what it is rather than what you wish it was or are afraid it is, you can make choices from a place of recovery.

How Reality May Become Distorted—and Perpetuate Toxic Relationships

Your wounding experiences, or trauma, have understandably impacted how you see yourself, others, and life in general, including the options available to you. Once your beliefs and perceptions have been wounded, your reality can become distorted in a number of ways that perpetuate toxic relationships. These distortions include:

- All-or-nothing thinking, including the idea that you (or your ex) are completely wrong or right, or that all people of a certain gender are the same.

- The illusion of inferiority/superiority, including the idea that you are "less than" others or "better than" others for any reason (remember, all human beings are inherently worthy and equal).
- The pattern of second-guessing yourself, which leaves you often feeling like you are "bad" or "wrong" for having needs, desires, or boundaries with others, or doubting what you *know* to be true.
- Numbing and disconnecting from reality, which includes a pattern of denial-based thoughts, such as "He didn't mean to do that or say that" or "What she really meant is..." and actively numbing from reality through substance use or other addictive behaviors like scrolling or overeating.
- Getting stuck in the idea that there is a "good" version of your partner and an unkind one —and that you have to work to make them the good version consistently (all of their behaviors are reality).
- The sunk cost fallacy, a psychological phenomenon where you believe that once you've put time, energy, or money into something, you cannot walk away because the reward is sure to follow eventually—even if this means investing extensive energy and effort "waiting" for the payoff. In toxic relationships, this manifests as the belief that your ideal relationship with your partner is *just* around the corner, compelling you to keep investing in it even if the objective facts show that this is extremely unlikely. For many, this also leads to the mistaken belief that if you leave now, someone else will reap all the benefits of your hard work making your partner "perfect."
- Social verification theory, which leads you to want to spend time with people who see you as poorly as you see yourself—or put you on a pedestal if you feel superior to others.
- The fantasy that another person can complete you (your wholeness comes from within you).
- The illusion that others have the ability to control or change you—or the mistaken belief that you have the right to control, change, or manipulate others.
- The belief that intensity, drama, both feeling "broken" in similar ways, and/or chaos in a relationship equates to passion, love, and being "soulmates."
- The illusion that safety is "boring."
- The false belief that you or others must be perfect to be lovable (human beings are inherently imperfect yet inherently worthy).

- The fantasy of being rescued—or saving another person (changing them to be who you want and having them live up to their "potential").
- The mental trap of a "trauma bond," which is the psychological phenomenon of feeling deeply connected to someone who abuses you—this person sadly becomes the perceived source of your relief when in reality they are the cause of your suffering.

All of these misperceptions of reality are understandable as they stem from wounding experiences. For example, it's completely understandable if you believe all women are cheaters because your ex cheated. Or that you believe control is love because you were neglected growing up. Yet these misperceptions of reality perpetuate toxic relationship patterns. It's like you become trapped in a hall of mirrors where you literally can't see the options available to you. It may look like automatically putting up walls on dates because you're afraid of being cheated on, which doesn't protect you but only repels healthy, securely attached potential partners. Or ignoring kind partners because their consistency and reliability seems "boring" when you've equated love with drama. To recover, you must become grounded in reality rather than living from your misperceptions. This wise place is where your core Self lives, and it's where safety is always available to you.

The Rescuer Fantasy

The rescuer fantasy is a common illusion for individuals stuck in toxic relationship cycles. There are two basic sides to the rescuer fantasy. The anxiously attached or codependent side of this fantasy centers on the idea that someone else can save you. This special person or "knight in shining armor" is seen as someone whose attention magically makes you worthy. For some, this misconception manifests as the belief that if someone "chooses" you, then you finally have proven your worth and your life now has meaning. Often this stems from abandonment and neglect wounds growing up.

Another version of the rescuer fantasy is the idea that a magical person out there may take away all your pain. Here, you may think if you find your "right" partner, they will make you feel so safe or happy that you'll never experience uncomfortable human emotions like loneliness or sadness again. Finally, another version of this illusion involves finding someone who completely provides for your physical rather than emotional needs. This is where the desire for a "sugar" daddy or mama comes in.

The flip side of this is the fantasy that you can be someone's rescuer. This "savior" may have an avoidant attachment style, where they approach relationships from a sense of obligation. They may enjoy taking care of others and even feel special being able to do so, yet they may still resent the other person's "neediness." They may use this resentment as fuel to reinforce their avoidant behaviors. A person with this sort of rescuer fantasy also likes to imagine themselves as completely independent and "together." They believe they are capable of taking care of others emotionally and/or materially without ever needing the same support. They are the "knight in shining armor" to the "damsel in distress" (of course, this gendered language obscures that people of all genders may take on the knight or damsel role). Their fantasy of personal perfection disconnects them from the vulnerability of being human. This may at times stem from wounding related to needing to perform for others, such as being the "little man" for mom when dad was away for work.

Other times, a person with anxious attachment wants to be the rescuer as a way of being needed and thereby never abandoned. They imagine that if someone is dependent on them, be it emotionally, physically, or financially, then they will never leave them. This person often has a deeply caring heart, but underneath their generosity is a desperate attempt to exchange caretaking for commitment. This hurts intimacy, though, because this type of rescuer may also try to take care of others by "fixing" or "saving" them in ways that feel harmful and controlling to the other person.

We can see both sides of the rescuer fantasy in the example of Mariane and Frederick.

• CASE STUDY: *Mariane and Frederick*

Mariane met Frederick when he was between jobs. She knew he had a lot of potential and was confident he'd figure it out soon. That's why when he asked to move in on their third date, she had no problem with it. However, over time, she realized that Frederick had no desire to actually get a job. He'd make lots of excuses about why he didn't apply for jobs every day when she'd come home from work: he was sick, he had a headache, his car wouldn't start, and so on. But she knew it was because he was addicted to video games. Mariane becomes resentful about paying all the bills and feeling used, but then Frederick makes big promises about how he'll go back to school or get a job. Mariane feels guilty for being "so hard" on him and drops it until she can't hold it in—repeating the cycle.

EXERCISE: Honoring Your Vulnerability

If you relate to aspects of the rescuer fantasy, this is understandable. This fantasy aims to cover up wounds related to being abandoned, rejected, neglected, or enmeshed growing up. When we imagine that we can save someone—or be rescued—it's a powerful mental illusion aiming to take away our fear, pain, longing, and insecurities. Yet, in reality, the rescuer illusion isn't truly soothing. After all, it's inherently disempowering. The rescuer/savior fantasy keeps you in a perpetual state of longing for someone or something else. Here, you need someone else to either "pick" you or to change in order to make your life feel complete. To support a greater sense of grounded wholeness *within yourself*, let's explore the ways this common fantasy may show up personally.

1. How does the rescuer fantasy show up for you? You may look to your past toxic relationship and what you most wanted from them to give you clues. If you wanted someone's constant attention, maybe you wanted to be rescued from feeling bored or insecure. Or if you always wanted to be in "control," this may be a sign you wanted to be the savior. Always thinking you are "right" is another sign of this.

____

____

____

____

2. Now imagine your fantasy becoming true. See it in as much detail as possible. Once you see this, remember that in human reality, there are always pros and cons. Remembering this truth, what potential limitations do you see with this fantasy coming true?

____

____

____

____

3. Now imagine your fantasy comes true but eventually there is a total one-eighty in events. What would you think or feel if you experienced the opposite reality? For example, your sugar "daddy" loses their money and is now dependent on you. Or if you suddenly are dependent due to a debilitating medical condition. What feelings or reactions would you have? While this may feel morbid, please remember that life is unpredictable and includes pain no matter how much we fantasize it won't. A securely attached person is one who is grounded in a sense of safety within themselves, weathering the changing tides of life maturely—not someone whose life is perfect.

____

____

____

____

4. Your fantasy reveals what you need from your Self. You must learn to provide yourself with the things you fantasize others must give you or how they need to change. If you want to be "rescued" from financial instability, you cultivate your own financial skills instead. Of if you constantly want "words of affirmation," you need to be more self-affirming. And if you always want to be "in control," it's important to practice self-compassion and self-soothing.

____

____

____

____

Example as Mariane

1. I want Frederick to live up to his true potential. I think I just need to give him time—and support—and he'll figure it out.
2. If he lives up to his potential, he will get a good, high-paying job. But I guess then he'll be busy, and I'll miss him.
3. I fantasize that I'll help him live up to his true potential. The opposite of this is that he doesn't have true potential. I would feel like such a fool for investing so much time, energy, and money into him then.
4. I need to support myself into living up to my "true" potential. I feel like life is just passing me by!

EXERCISE: Coping Well with Vulnerability

Life holds tremendous uncertainty, including the fact that setbacks, changes to our physical bodies, and the deaths of ourselves and loved ones are unavoidable. To be alive is to be vulnerable to the ever-changing tides of life—one moment there is joy, and another, pain. The rescuer fantasy acts to pacify the discomfort from the vulnerability in being alive. And yet, no matter how much a person clings to this fantasy, you and all other human beings are inherently vulnerable. To truly soothe yourself well in the face of this uncomfortable uncertainty, it helps to cope from a place of grounded wholeness. Here, you tap into the fact that you *already* can cope well with this vulnerability as your Self, who unconditionally holds you through life's ups and downs. You will practice this now.

1. Your wise Self knows vulnerability is a natural part of life and cannot be eradicated. Rather than waving a magic wand, the securely attached parent soothes the child when they're overwhelmed or uncertain. One way to do this is by supporting resiliency in the child. You can do this in numerous ways, including noticing your interconnection with all other people. Consider how you are supported in innumerable ways. What was the last meal you ate? Note all the effort you can think of that other people invested for you to have this food, such as the farmers, grocery store employees, and drivers.

2. A sense of connection to something greater than yourself, such as a sense of purpose or a higher power, supports resiliency. Your Self may be considered your soul or the essence of your consciousness, which may wisely guide you to a sense of purpose. Perhaps you find this through a belief in God (or the Universe or your "higher self"), which gives your life meaning and direction. Or maybe you find this in meaningful work or relationships. What are your personal beliefs about being connected to something greater than yourself? This doesn't need to be religious and may simply be noticing the communities you are a part of at this time, or nature. How do these beliefs support you?

3. Moving forward, when the rescuer/rescued fantasy arises in your mind, please comfort yourself as your securely attached Self rather than looking outside of yourself for relief. Consider a word or image that represents your interconnectedness and your sense of purpose. Draw or write that here:

4. Gently tap your heart center with your fingertips as you repeat this word or visualize the image. Come back to this word or image whenever your nonsecurely attached part is triggered into the rescuer fantasy.

Example as Mariane

1. I had coffee and a banana. People halfway across the world whom I'll never meet and be able to thank grew the coffee beans and the banana tree that produced my meal. Oh—and someone grew and harvested the cashews for my coffee creamer.
2. I believe there is something greater than myself, but I don't know what. However, I've had experiences like my grandma visiting me in my dream after she died that felt real. I've wanted to learn more about spirituality. To support myself, I'll read the book I bought on this topic sitting on my shelf. I'll also remember that I'm still connected to my grandma even though she's gone, the people in my city, and really people even across the world growing my food. I can remember this in the future when I think Frederick has to live up to his "potential" for me to feel complete.
3. "Complete."

Finding Proof for Your Beliefs

Another way people commonly distort reality is by looking for proof of what they already believe rather than keeping an open mind. In toxic relationships, the beliefs people often look to validate are rooted in trauma. For instance, all-or-nothing beliefs about others, such as "all women are gold diggers" or "all men are immature," are typically the result of wounding. The same is true for all-or-nothing beliefs about yourself, such as "I'm unlovable" or "I'm always right." These wounds then lead parts of you to seek validation of these painful beliefs rather than seeing the expansive truth of reality. Your wounds obfuscate the truth that while some women may seek money over love, or some men may be childish, there are many women and men who aren't like this. Nonsecure, wounded parts often lean toward the psychological phenomenon called confirmation bias. Here people look for proof of what they already believe and discard any information that contradicts these established views. This confirmation bias reinforces nonsecure attachment and toxic relationship cycles.

Toxic Relationships Can Verify Your Self-Concept

You, like all people, carry a concept of yourself. For people with enough supportive and reliable experiences with others, they carry a secure view of self. They know they are imperfect yet lovable. They trust they are worth others' time and attention and feel comfortable providing this to others. Yet trauma disconnects many of us from our inherent, equal worth and value to all others. And sadly, the human tendency toward confirmation bias may lead you to reinforce these painful beliefs.

Sometimes to cope with their wounding, a person makes up—and compulsively demonstrates—that they are superior to others. They may perform as being better through money, intelligence, or their bodies as examples. These people are more likely to be avoidantly attached. Other times, a person's wounds mistakenly cause them to believe they are less than others, which causes an anxious attachment style. In either case, these people are disconnected from their inherent and equal worth as imperfect human beings.

In toxic relationships, people often seek to reinforce their illusions of superiority or inferiority. Social verification theory explains how people prefer to be with others who see them in the same way they see themselves. This congruency in self-view and how another person sees them makes them feel comfortable. On the other hand, spending time with people who see them differently than their self-concept creates discomfort. This is true even when it doesn't make sense logically. For instance, if a person believes "I'm not good enough," this theory explains how they'll pursue someone who also believes they are "not good enough." While painful, a dating partner thinking as poorly about you as you do may seem comfortable in its familiarity. Furthermore, it's often easier to trust someone who verifies your self-concept. If you think you are "worthless," a person seeing your innate talents and beauty may seem untrustworthy or even repulsive.

Social verification also helps explain why finding yourself in a toxic or abusive relationship has nothing to do with intelligence. For instance, survivors of sexual abuse often feel they must exchange sex for attention, and sometimes they misconstrue sexual violence, including coercion, as "normal" because of their histories (Steil, Schneider, and Schwartzkopff 2022). Sadly, social verification theory makes it more likely a survivor will partner with someone who feels entitled to sex and who mistreats them otherwise.

EXERCISE: Becoming a Positive Reality Detective

Your life experiences and relationships have naturally shaped the way you see yourself, others, and life in general. Sometimes, these views are helpful, such as believing in your capabilities due to positive feedback growing up. (Of course, sometimes such positive attention can inadvertently make us believe that we *only* have value when we are achieving.) Other times, these views may perpetuate toxic cycles. In this exercise, you'll explore how confirming some of your beliefs interferes with your recovery. If you have only an anxious or avoidant attachment style, you will complete the relevant steps. Otherwise, if you have an anxious-avoidant attachment style, please complete all the steps.

1. **If you have an anxious attachment style**, identify your greatest fear or something you worry about when it comes to potential partners, such as "Only people I don't want, want me." Put that fear in the middle of the first circle below. (If avoidant only, please go to step 5.)

2. Now, draw lines from this circle to provide examples that validate this belief to you as true.

3. What would you like to believe instead? Write that more supportive belief in the second circle.

4. Drawing lines from this circle, provide proof of this new, more positive belief. Act like a detective to be as thorough as possible, looking for proof of this belief.

5. **If you have an avoidant attachment style**, consider what you believe about potential partners and how they see you, such as "I'm so attractive I can treat men however I want."

6. Based on this belief, consider how you treat the people you date. Draw lines from the circle to write these examples. Also draw lines for how this belief may negatively impact you.

7. Acting securely attached requires mutual respect. What would be a belief to support this? Write this in the other circle.

8. Draw lines from this new, healthier belief with proof of how you may already act this way. Additionally, provide examples of more ways to act on this new belief and how this would make you feel.

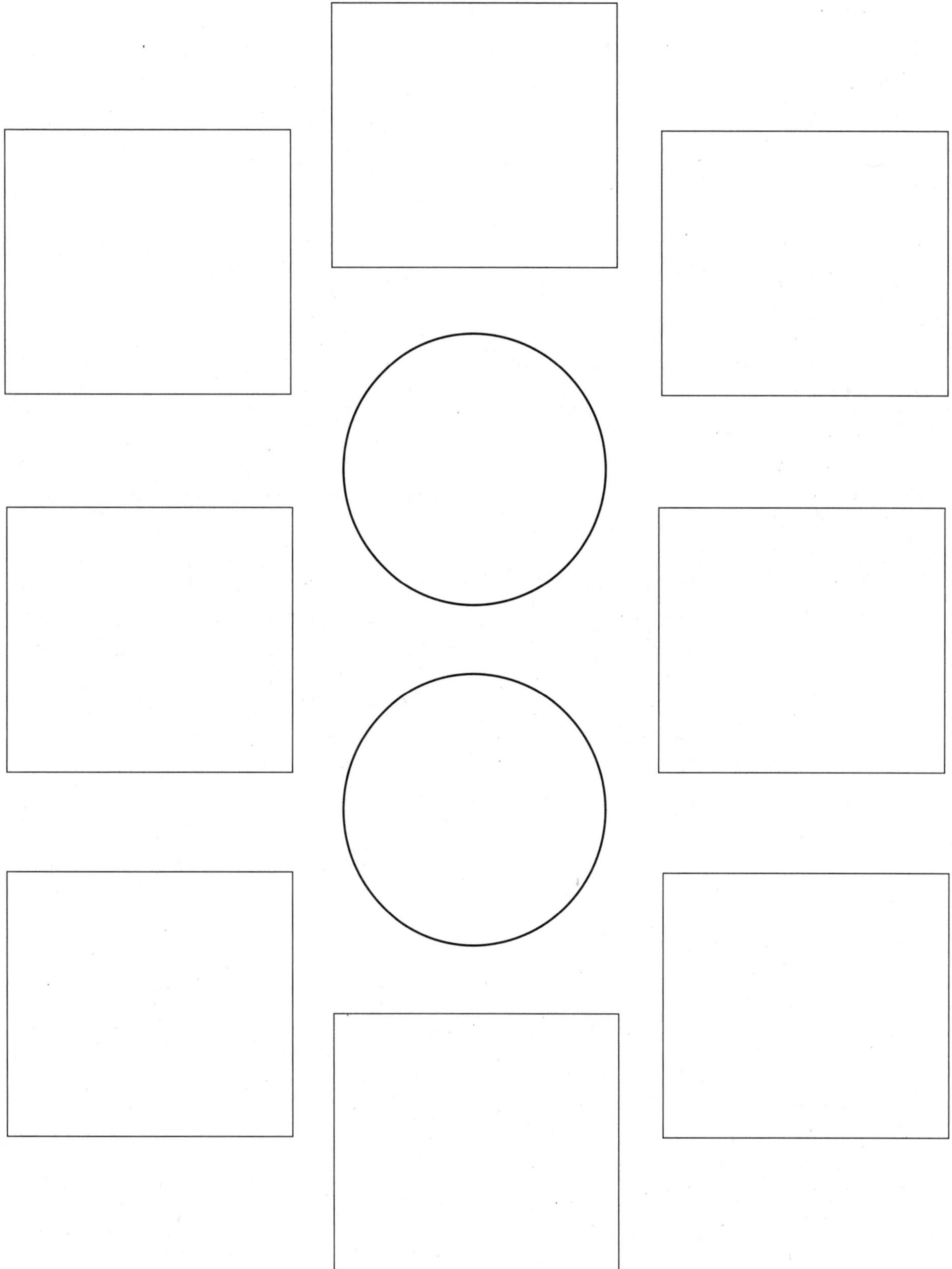

EXAMPLE AS MARIANE

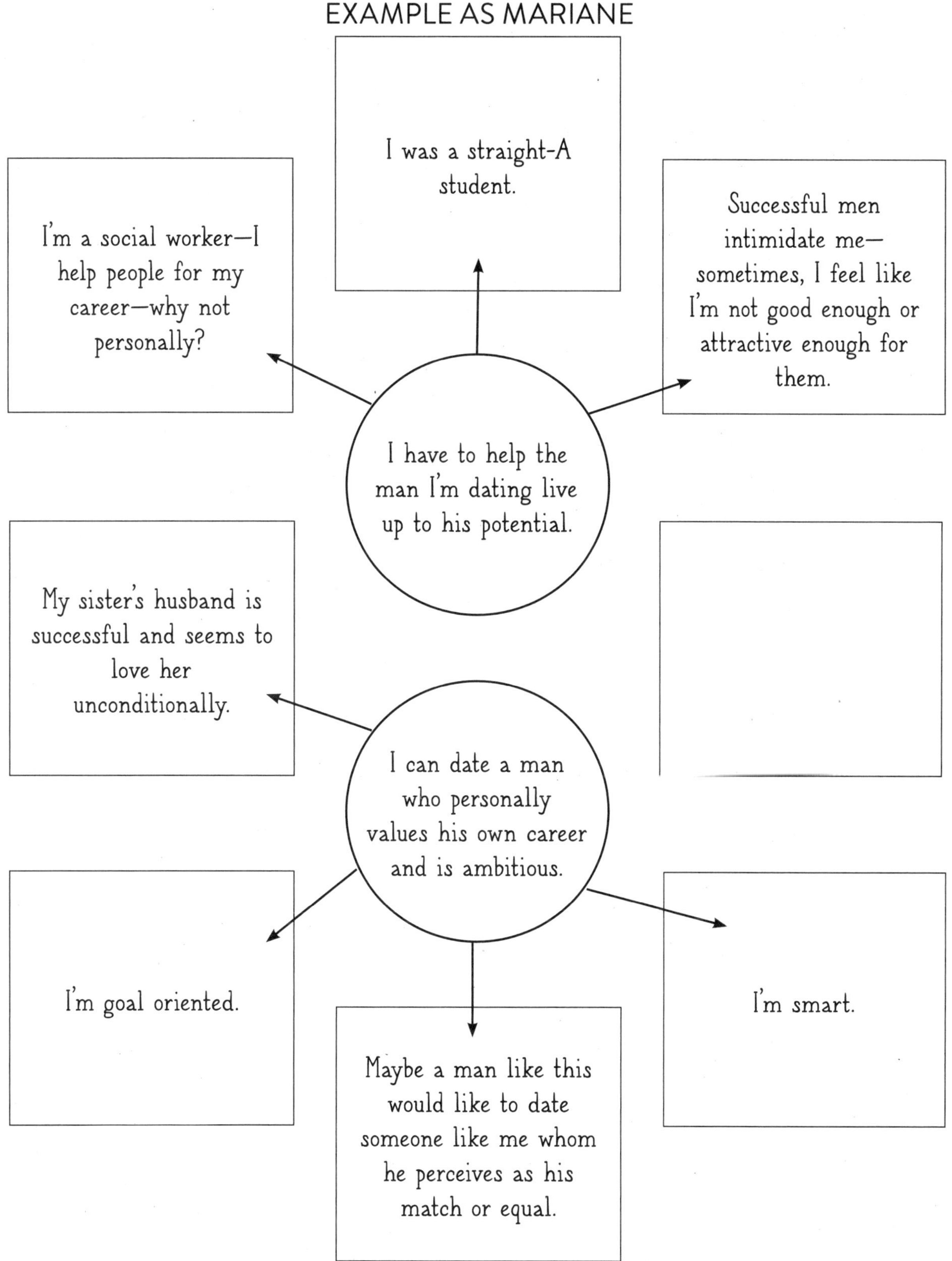

Waiting for Someone to Change

Commonly in toxic relationships, an anxiously attached person will deny the reality of someone's character. They tolerate mistreatment and the other person's unwillingness to meet their needs due to the misconception that the other person will eventually change. They also sadly equate someone's willingness, or unwillingness, to change with their worth. Complicating this, they often believe if they walk away, their partner will suddenly change, leaving their next partner to reap the benefits of all their hard work. They prioritize their partner's imagined potential over who they really are. This fantasy is rooted in the sunk cost fallacy, which, as we've discussed, is the mistaken belief that because you have deeply invested in something, you can't abandon it. A classic example is the gambler who is convinced that every "next time" will be their big win, so they can't stop now.

Unfortunately, when someone is disconnected from reality, they often prioritize words over actions. They may spend countless hours trying to understand why their partner says one thing but does something else. They will often rationalize and justify their partner's actions too. For instance, "He says he loves me, but he calls me names. I guess that's just because it's what he saw his dad do." Or "She must've ghosted me because she's so overwhelmed by the intensity of our connection."

People say "Talk is cheap," but in reality, talk is literally free. Securely attached people understand this and prioritize actions over words, without personalizing other people's choices as a sign of their worth or lack thereof. While they appreciate compliments, they know it's someone's character and actions that provide the foundation of a healthy relationship rather than empty words. Finally, they have healthy boundaries, which means they both self-protect and respect others. They know it's a boundary violation to try to change others for their "potential," even if well-meaning.

Being Grounded in Reality

People in toxic relationships often feel disconnected from reality not only mentally but also physically. Nonsecure attachment originating from relationship trauma leads many people to feel numb or cold. Sometimes, avoidant clients say they feel robotic. They may *know* they love someone, but they can't feel the warmth of this love inside. Other times, especially after abusive relationships, clients will say they no longer feel "human."

This physical self-disconnection then perpetuates toxic relationship patterns. For example, while anxiously attached people tend to *feel a lot*, it's often in imbalanced empathy for the other person, as previously discussed. Ironically, they're often numb to their own feelings. This numbness reinforces clinging to unkind or unavailable partners. Otherwise, if they could literally *feel* how much the other person hurts them deeply and consistently, they'd be more compelled to leave.

On the other hand, avoidantly attached people are enabled to continue using, manipulating, or pushing partners away through this physical disconnection. A sense of being emotionally dead prevents them from feeling the natural consequences of pain, shame, guilt, empathy, and love when they hurt another person, especially one they claim to care about.

A sense of being dissociated, which means feeling "out of your body," numb, or frozen, is a natural physiological response to trauma. If you often feel like you're not "here" in your body in your life, this is a sign you may be dissociative at times. Sometimes a person also stops feeling like they, others, or their lives are "real." This is called depersonalization. A sign of this disconnection from reality is dating people for the "story" you get to tell others rather than prioritizing the impact someone is having on you.

EXERCISE: Grounding into Reality

Grounding into reality is how you break out of the illusions that perpetuate toxic relationships. A great question for this is, "What's really going on right now outside of my illusions, fears, projections, fantasies, and insecurities?" But to hear this answer, sometimes you need mindful time to be present with your overwhelmed, scared, or numb parts. Know that if you have parts that feel numb, frozen, or unreal, there is nothing "wrong" with you; these are natural responses to trauma. And you can heal by learning to focus on your mind-body connection. The mind is a helpful tool, but you cannot learn to feel again by intellectualizing this process. Instead, you must be willing to feel your sensations, which include hunger and thirst as well as what the mind labels as emotions. To help, practice embodying activities such as dancing, yoga, using a weighted blanket, self-massage, or breath work. Simply being aware of the water on your skin when you shower or truly tasting your food helps too. You already began to practice mindful presence in your body. Here, you will deepen this.

1. If you feel comfortable, take off your shoes. Go outside on bare earth if this is available to you. If not, simply being barefoot on tile is great too.

2. Place your bare feet on the ground while standing (if this is not an option, you may do this seated) and wiggle your toes to orient your attention to your feet. Notice your whole body being supported by the ground.

3. Now you may notice you have a lot of scattered mental energy, such as feeling distracted or judging. If so, imagine reclaiming your scattered energy and pulling it back into your body. It may feel like warmth or look like light. You may envision putting your energy into your feet almost like putting a sock on in reverse.

4. Wonderful! Now scan your body for any tension. Make sure to check your back, neck, and shoulders, as these are commonly tense areas.

5. If you're tense, breathe deeply and imagine pushing the tension out of your body into the ground with your exhalation. Repeat this process of releasing your tension into the ground for at least three to five deep belly breaths.

6. Great job. Now scan your chest for any pressure or tightness. See if you can become aware of any blocks in your heart space to feeling your own emotions and/or feeling your impact on others. Breathe, seeing how these blocks form a wall preventing you from *feeling* love for yourself and/or others.

7. Inhale, imagining the warmth of your breath melting away any parts of this wall you're ready to release today. Let the tension and pressure go by breathing this energy through your torso, hips, legs, feet, and into the ground.

8. Take a gentle breath, affirming you are safe to feel love because you know how to assess danger accurately while accepting healthy love.

9. Wonderful job. Repeat this exercise whenever you feel numb.

EXERCISE: Surrendering to Reality

A good way to become more grounded is to honor the truth that your body has literal needs. Often, when people are in toxic relationship cycles, their self-care goes by the wayside. Here you'll honor your body's literal needs like an attentive, consistently nurturing parent. Reliably self-soothing when you're distressed and consistently self-caring are essential for recovery. It's also a tangible way you can be rescued by your Self, or you can save the right person—yourself!

1. All bodies require basic care, even though it can be easy to put these needs on the back burner. Compassionately circle the ways you may currently neglect your basic needs. Please remember it's understandable why you may currently neglect this, *and* you're empowered to evolve:

   - Moving my body
   - Eating nourishing food
   - Getting enough sleep
   - Drinking enough water
   - Resting

2. Next to anything you circle, validate why it makes sense that you currently deprioritize this, such as by staying up late because you want some "me" time.

3. With understanding, notice that a healthy parent is nurturing, which includes setting limits on activities that harm you. They don't let their child eat candy endlessly and stay up all

night; you must do the same for yourself. You know that while these things feel good in the moment, the long-term consequences aren't worth the momentary pleasure. Consider one small change you can implement to care for any needs you currently deprioritize. Write this commitment to one area you may currently self-neglect.

____

____

____

____

Please make these very simple for now; for example, drink one glass of water when I get to work, walk around my block at lunch, and eat a piece of fruit daily. Then set reminders on your phone to support yourself in staying committed.

Grounding into Reality for Security
Chapter Reminders

Great job connecting more with reality in order to overcome the ways distorted thinking sometimes perpetuates toxic relationship cycles! To support you moving forward, please remember:

- Disconnection from reality—including thinking errors like all-or-nothing thoughts, sunk cost fallacy, and social verification—explain why you may have perpetuated toxic relationship patterns in the past.
- By being aware of these distortions of reality, you are empowered to interrupt them to see reality more clearly, such as by challenging your confirmation bias.
- These beliefs that perpetuate toxic relationships are often rooted in trauma—you can challenge them *and* maintain self-compassion.
- Grounding into reality by becoming more present to your body's sensations and literal needs allows you to recover.

Chapter 8

CULTIVATING HEALTHY RELATIONSHIP SKILLS

In this chapter, you will now focus on some of the essential skills of having a healthy relationship with another person. It may seem strange that we've waited until this point to cultivate these skills, yet it's intentional. The reality is, every relationship you have with another person is founded on how compassionately connected you are with yourself. While it's not true that you can't love another person until you love yourself, it is true that you can only love another person to the extent that you truly love your authentic, whole Self.

Aspects of your self-relationship that support your healthy, securely attached relationship with others include:

- Your commitment to being self-aware and honest with yourself about your emotions, nonsecure triggers, needs, wants, and limits
- Your practice of consistent self-care and self-soothing to effectively manage distressing emotions, which are present even in the healthiest of relationships, since these emotions are part of being alive
- Practicing courage to communicate kindly and directly about needs and limits to protect yourself and the relationship
- Your balanced self-interest, which includes appropriately giving and receiving support and grace

By staying committed to honoring these aspects of your relationship with yourself, you create a space for a truly balanced, intimate, securely attached relationship. The skills in this chapter support you in having a healthy relationship in general. You can begin to cultivate these now as you recover from your toxic relationship, even if you're currently single. Please know the skills covered in this chapter are an introduction to those needed in a securely attached, healthy relationship. Here you are planting seeds you'll continue to cultivate and grow throughout your entire life. A truly healthy relationship requires ongoing commitment to your personal skills. To support you with your ongoing practice, see the Resources section at the end of this workbook.

Toxic Relationships and Extremes

In your toxic relationship, you likely struggled to find a sense of balance or interdependency. Common ways this imbalance shows up in a relationship are:

- The way anger is expressed
- Discomfort with the reality of conflict in a relationship
- An all-or-nothing relationship with boundaries

- Difficulty coping with the inevitability of fear when it arises in a close relationship
- Struggling to find a sense of equality around the need for both give and take in a close relationship

In your toxic relationship, you likely acted in extreme ways more often than balanced ones. After all, both avoidant and anxious attachment reside in the extremes of self-worth and treatment of others. If you're anxiously attached, you tend to be too self-less by consistently prioritizing others' needs and preferences over your needs, wants, and limits. You likely feel guilty if you feel angry, need to set a boundary, or change your mind about something. If you're avoidantly attached, you may have a pattern of being too self-full by consistently prioritizing your fears, needs, wants, and walls over others. At times, this may lead to a sense of entitlement to special treatment. For example, you may expect others to *not* set boundaries with you that they may need to protect themselves from your hurtful behaviors. This sometimes manifests in the attitude that "if you can't handle me at my worst, you don't deserve me at my best," regardless of how this treatment hurts the other person.

Either imbalanced approach is related to trauma, though, and you are not bad for acting in these ways. To survive your past wounding, you may have silenced yourself to try to keep others calm or happy. Alternatively, you may have needed to imagine you were more special than others as a sort of emotional armor to survive your trauma. While understandable, you may now break free from these behaviors, which unwittingly perpetuate toxic relationships.

Coping Well with Anger

Conflict is inevitable in any relationship despite the common fantasy that with your "right" person there will never be misunderstanding. However, research shows 69 percent of problems in a romantic partnership are unsolvable (Gottman 2011). This means the majority of problems cannot be solved, regardless of your choice in partner. The only difference is that when you exchange one partner for another, you acquire a different set of unsolvable problems. Common unsolvable problems include having different values around money, parenting, time with extended family, and how often partners enjoy socializing with others. To have a truly healthy, thriving, securely attached long-term relationship, it's essential to find a person with whom you can consistently and authentically negotiate these unsolvable problems. This means being clear on the things you *cannot* negotiate around to be true to yourself. For example, if you authentically want to get married or have kids but your partner doesn't, you will always be self-sacrificing your core desires to stay with this person. This sort of sacrifice is what a nonsecurely attached person attempts to accept—but ultimately can't, as these needs are nonnegotiable. Even if you stay with this person, there will typically be a constant, underlying sense of sadness, regret, and resentment. A securely attached person will absolutely grieve this relationship where there is an inherent incompatibility, but they don't deny the reality of their needs *or* try to manipulate their partner into changing. They know these irreconcilable differences are no one's fault, but they are willing to let go and free each other up to live authentically.

However, in toxic relationships, couples often get stuck in how they negotiate around unsolvable problems. They'll deny essential incompatibilities, trying to change one another. Or they get stuck in power struggles around the things they'd *prefer* but that aren't nonnegotiables for them. For example, let's say you *prefer* your partner is more affectionate, but it's not honestly, authentically a deal-breaker. In a securely attached relationship, when someone's differences don't violate you on a core level, you work to love them in an unconditionally accepting way instead.

In healthy, secure partnerships, you accept that conflict is natural. You are two separate people with different needs and values, and even a healthy partner will trigger feelings of anger at times. In fact, because of the importance of close attachments, the people closest to you most intensely trigger your anger—and fear. These emotions are acceptable, yet your urges may be hurtful. The urge of anger is to be destructive—yell, throw things, or say cruel words. And yet, when you practice healthy relationship skills, you choose to cope well with your anger instead. By doing this, you are then better equipped to negotiate with your partner, which is the essential skill for managing unsolvable problems.

Finally, please remember that while anger and conflict are unavoidable, abuse is never acceptable. If you constantly have to walk on eggshells because a partner is cruel and destructive, this is not okay. Some people are unwilling to not be abusive regardless of how much personal work you do. This is not a reflection of your worth, just a painful truth. In such relationships, you may need to leave to have the chance to experience healthy conflict with someone else.

Let's look at the example of Natasha and Monique to see how the way you deal with anger can be the difference between a toxic relationship and a healthy one.

• CASE STUDY: *Natasha and Monique*

Natasha runs hot and cold in her relationships. When she first meets someone she likes, she becomes obsessive. The relationship usually moves very quickly with declarations of love and spending all their time together. When they can't be together, Natasha tends to second-guess the relationship at first. She constantly checks her phone for messages, and if they "take too long" to reply, she feels despair. However, after a few months, she suddenly becomes angry that her partner wants to be with her so much. But instead of communicating directly, she stops returning calls or texts and is suddenly "too busy" to hang out. Natasha is presently doing this to Monique, her current partner. When Monique asks Natasha to hang out, Natasha feels angry and repulsed by Monique's "desperation." Natasha is now looking for someone new—someone better, in her mind—on a dating app. She's hoping Monique will just get the message she's not interested in her anymore.

EXERCISE: Balancing Your Anger to Protect Your Relationship

The practice of coping well with anger requires you to mindfully acknowledge when you feel angry while also calming yourself enough to be kind to the other person. It's natural to forget exactly how to effectively self-soothe when you're angry. In this exercise, you'll be introduced to an emotional tool kit that can help you interrupt this pattern.

Before we get into the steps of self-soothing, first think about a recent time that you were angry. Describe that experience in as much detail as possible here. We'll refer to this experience throughout the exercise to practice the steps of self-soothing.

____

____

____

____

____

Being Mindful of When You're Dysregulated (in Fight-or-Flight)

1. Your nervous system becomes dysregulated when you feel angry. Without soothing yourself as soon as possible, you may naturally respond to the situation in fight-or-flight. These natural responses to anger can hurt yourself and the relationship if left unchecked, so it's important to soothe the anger as soon as possible. To do this, you first need to be mindful of your physical signs of anger. What are your personal cues to anger? Circle any you relate to while adding your own:

   - Seeing red
   - Heart racing
   - Shallow breathing
   - Holding my breath
   - Panic
   - Sweaty palms
   - Feeling physically hot
   - Jaw tension
   - Fists clenching
   - Wanting to punch or throw something
   - Pouting my lips
   - My blood burning

In the experience you wrote about above, what anger cues do you remember experiencing?

____

____

____

____

2. When you feel your anger cues, take a self-soothing break. If you're having a conversation with somebody when you feel yourself getting angry, let them know you need a break and step away. Then choose a calming activity to help comfort yourself. It's really important to choose soothing activities when you're angry because activities like jogging or punching something actually "turn up the heat" on your anger—we want to cool the heat down (Kjærvik and Bushman 2024).

   Circle the activities in the following list that most interest you for quick support next time you're angry. Also, you may "layer" soothing activities, like giving yourself a massage with essential oil while listening to nature sounds.

   - Breathe deeply, visualizing breathing out anger and breathing in calm or breathing in for a count of four and out for a count of five
   - Practice 5 to 10 minutes of gentle yoga, perhaps using YouTube or another guide
   - Progressively relax your muscles: start at the top of your head and release your scalp, then move through each body part, imagining releasing tension in each place
   - Do a guided meditation to release anger and feel peace
   - Take a slow, mindful nature walk (even around your block, looking for as many flowers as possible)
   - Sit on the earth and look at the sky
   - Take a cool shower or bath (not too hot, as this will be activating)
   - Give yourself a massage
   - Listen to calming music (not too energizing, as this is activating) or nature sounds
   - Hold an ice cube in your hand until it melts (or you can no longer tolerate it)
   - Use calming essential oils like lavender, rose, lemon, or vetiver

3. When you were experiencing anger, did you choose any self-soothing activities? If not, which ones do you think could have been useful?

4. Validate yourself as a securely attached parent. Thinking about the experience you wrote about above, express *why* it makes sense you felt this way and that your anger was natural. Write these kind, understanding words here:

5. Honor your anger by letting your inner child express themselves. Still thinking of the example from earlier in this exercise, draw a picture of what this anger looked like. Remember to be compassionate and avoid perfectionism. You are simply expressing yourself right now, and there's no one to judge, including you!

6. To complete this exercise, do something soothing for yourself—it can be from the list above or something else that sounds relaxing or calming. You will come back to this important information you've cultivated shortly.

Protecting Yourself and the Relationship with Healthy Boundaries

A balanced, securely attached relationship requires the cultivation of healthy boundaries. There are two parts to healthy boundaries:

1. The external limits we need to set with others to feel safe and respected
2. The internal limits we need to set on ourselves as our core Self acting as a securely attached parent, to be safe and respectful to others

These limits ensure that through a sense of healthy separation from others, we can connect more deeply. It is only when we set healthy boundaries with others while respecting their limits that we can experience the depths of profound intimacy. Getting here, of course, is a practice for all of us, but nonsecure attachment complicates this process.

Unfortunately, many people with a nonsecure attachment style have an all-or-nothing relationship with boundaries. An avoidantly attached person may hide behind walls, for example. They also may have a lessened sense of accountability and empathy toward others. This means they may not set the limits on themselves they need to be safe for others. For example, if they have the urge to use someone for attention, sex, or money, they won't interrupt this. They may use others for their own benefit, which is a boundary violation.

On the other hand, an anxiously attached person may be so afraid of abandonment that they won't honor even their most basic needs. For instance, they may feel guilty for saying "no" to requests even when it's not possible for them. Or they may wonder whether they're "asking for too much" when they want basic respect. Rather than having no boundaries and potentially feeling like a "doormat," or building walls, the healthy middle ground is to have consistent yet flexible boundaries. To help, you may imagine a flexible bubble that protects you at all times. You are not cut off from others. At the same time, you don't have to carry others' feelings and expectations. This balanced approach to boundaries includes self-respect and other-respect. Many salvageable relationships have been deemed "irreconcilable" simply because couples weren't willing to be balanced in how they respect themselves *and* their partner.

EXERCISE: Honoring the Gift of Your Anger

While you may have learned that anger is scary or unacceptable, anger provides a tremendous gift for healthy relationships. This gift is letting you know your boundaries and needs in a relationship. This is because when a need is unmet or a boundary is violated, it's natural to feel angry, even if you're not consciously aware of these needs or limits.

In this activity, you will practice using your anger to identify a boundary and communicating it.

1. Go back to the previous exercise. You did a great job soothing yourself as a loving, securely attached parent. Now, it's time to receive the gift in your anger. To communicate well, you must first identify your need or boundary. Based on the situation you described, what does your inner child need? Practice compassion and empathy for your anger.

   ____

   ____

   ____

2. Now you have the opportunity to act securely with yourself—and as a responsible, mature adult toward someone else—by owning your emotions and needs directly. A simple way to communicate directly involves telling the other person how you feel using an "I" statement. However, please avoid saying "I feel like" or "I feel that," as these express thoughts and interpretations rather than emotions. When you express interpretations rather than emotions, it's more likely you'll receive a defensive response. Rather, you want to own your authentic emotions.

   First, list your emotion.

   I feel ____________________________________

   ____

   Then list the facts like a fly on the wall would see it.

   In this situation, ________________________________

   ____

Finally, express your needs in a sentence or two. Keeping it short will help you avoid a common behavior of justifying yourself with a list of reasons, which can be overwhelming and distract from your boundaries.

I need or want ______________________________

____

3. Take the steps to assert this limit. It's okay to be scared. You may have the urge to suppress your needs; that's okay, and you can still change. Fundamentally, changing your attachment style is simply about being willing to change your nonsecurely attached behaviors. Write out what you'd like to say to your partner ahead of talking to them.

____

____

____

4. Once you've communicated your limits, take time to listen to the other person. Compromise where you can, but please, don't give up your boundaries if they're challenged. If you need extra support, there's an online tool for this workbook on how to respond if your boundaries are disregarded, which you can access at http://www.newharbinger.com/55992. You cannot have a healthy relationship without respecting your own needs.

Example as Natasha

I feel overwhelmed and annoyed that you want to hang out and talk every day. I know that for the first three months we were together most nights; however, my work has been slipping, and I haven't been getting enough rest. I need more "me" time by only having a couple of date nights a week right now. I understand this change makes you anxious, but by respecting my need for my time, I believe we will be able to develop a healthier, longer relationship together.

Coping Well with Fear

At the root of all nonsecure attachment is fear, whether it's conscious or not. This is clear with anxious attachment and its core fears of loss, abandonment, and rejection. But avoidant attachment is also rooted in fear—the fear of intimacy rather than isolation. Furthermore, avoidantly attached people also naturally fear loss, but they respond by pushing away closeness to not get too attached, rather than clinging to closeness.

To cope with these fears, many people develop patterns of interacting with a partner that are unhelpful. For instance, an anxious person may try to control their partner. They may try to get their partner to hold back certain parts of themselves out of their jealousy or insecurity. For example, something as simple as a partner wanting a night with friends may trigger these controlling tendencies in an anxious partner. Or an avoidant partner may shut down to these insecurities and become distant, saying, for example, "It's fine you want a night out with friends. In fact, I think you should just go somewhere for a week with them. I'm fine by myself!"

Securely attached people are still afraid of loss, rejection, abandonment, and uncertainty. They are human, after all. But they cope with these fears in helpful rather than unhelpful ways. Sadly, the ways a nonsecurely attached person copes with their fear tend to reinforce anxiety and insecurity. For instance, an avoidantly attached person will try to protect themselves by building walls and being emotionally closed off out of a fear of intimacy or difficulty trusting others. And yet these walls only reinforce their fears, preventing them from cultivating deeper trust with another. Then, when a partner responds naturally to their walls with sadness or anger, the avoidantly attached person will take this as "proof" they can't trust others to not suffocate them. And when an anxiously attached person clings or controls out of a fear of abandonment, this tends to repel others. It's natural a partner will tire of the emotional labor of constantly reassuring an anxiously attached partner. This becomes exhausting for most people when the anxiously attached person's fear is never quelled.

The pathway out of these nonsecure reactions to fear is to love courageously. The creator of Internal Family Systems, Richard Schwartz, explains, "When each partner has courageous love for the other, many of the chronic struggles most couples face melt away because each partner is released from being primarily responsible for making the other feel good. Instead, each knows how to care for their own vulnerability, so neither has to force the other into a preconceived mold or control the other's journey" (2023).

EXERCISE: Embracing Vulnerability

To cope well with fear, you must practice tolerating vulnerability despite feeling uncomfortable. Embracing vulnerability involves accepting the natural uncertainty of relationships, accepting support, and showing up as your authentic, valuable, and imperfect self. Vulnerability is the basis of profound intimacy. This activity helps you show up vulnerably in a balanced, safe way.

1. When you feel overwhelmed, out of control, or anxious in a relationship, how have you coped with this previously? Circle any behaviors you relate to while adding any you know of not listed here:

    - Pushing the person away
    - Obsessing about what the other person thinks or feels and constantly analyze their words and actions
    - Becoming really busy
    - Cheating
    - Ghosting
    - Wanting constant contact
    - Asking for constant reassurance
    - Breaking up with them before they could break up with me
    - Trying to control them, such as how often they go out or drink
    - Avoiding important necessary conversations, such as to set a boundary or establish commitment
    - Obsessing about when I last received communication from them
    - Justifying mistreatment (including making excuses for them) because I'm afraid of being alone
    - Getting stuck in self- or other-criticism

2. It's natural to catastrophize when we are afraid. This is when we obsess about the worst-case scenario happening. In what ways do you find yourself catastrophizing? What is the worst-case scenario you've been imagining?

    ____

    ____

    ____

3. Sometimes, your perception of what's unsafe and safe for you may become confused, as you learned in chapter 4. When this happens, at times you may exaggerate a threat. Other times,

your mind may ignore or deny a threat to your safety. Does what you are imagining as the worst-case scenario match the facts of the situation?

____

____

4. If you're currently unsafe, for example, you are dating someone who's attacking you or cheating on you, what boundaries can you set to protect yourself? You may not be ready to set the boundary of outright leaving, and that's okay; give yourself grace. What steps can you take to protect yourself, such as creating a separate savings account so you have the option to leave if you decide to do so later to protect yourself?

____

____

____

____

____

5. Whether you are safe or unsafe, it's time to nurture your scared parts. Comfort yourself with affirmations, such as "It's okay to not like vulnerability and I can be brave." Validate that it's natural to feel scared, saying, for example, "It's natural to be afraid this relationship you're investing time in may not work out. But you won't know whether this is the right person for you without investing more time and energy into it. Whatever happens with this person, I'll be here for you." Write down your affirmation:

____

____

____

6. Great job; now take a moment to soothe yourself. Take a few deep breaths, and if you're willing, wrap your arms around yourself. Give yourself a hug (or place one hand on your heart and one hand on your belly). Repeat your affirmation. Remember, it's scary to be human sometimes. It's really vulnerable to be alive! And courage is necessary to achieve the sense of security you desire.

7. You're doing a wonderful job showing up for yourself safely! Now, are there any things you may do to show up as a safe person for someone else, even if you feel afraid? For example, you may work to be more honest about your needs or concerns with someone rather than isolating.

____

____

____

Example as Natasha

1. I cheat, ghost, and want constant contact and reassurance.
2. I'm afraid I'll be alone for the rest of my life.
3. No, it's not accurate to assume I'll be alone for the rest of my life. It only feels like this because it's been a self-fulfilling prophecy; as soon as someone gets too close, I push them away.
4. I'm not unsafe. Just scared and vulnerable that I've been with Monique for four months now.
5. "I want a relationship in my life. I can be brave and learn to start communicating directly to move past the initial first few months with someone."
6. "I can be brave."
7. I need to give my relationship with Monique some time now that she respected my need for just a couple of date nights per week. It's truly too soon to tell whether we're a long-term match, but she's respecting me, and I do like her.

EXERCISE: Opening Yourself Up to Receiving

Nonsecurely attached people tend to struggle with receiving. Commonly, the vulnerability of receiving triggers insecurities. These include the fear of being disappointed later on, fear of being manipulated, or insecurity around deserving kindness. Other times, a person may feel entitled to receive, which leads them to take from others in an imbalanced way. This is different from genuine receptivity, which is humble and grateful.

Because you have inherent and equal worth to all other human beings, you never have to "prove," "earn," or "deserve" joyful, good experiences or things. Simply because you're alive, you have the birthright to receive kindness and support from others. At the same time, as others are equally special and important, you are not entitled to more love, support, or generosity. Part of forging healthy connections is allowing yourself to receive, as it's not intimate to put up walls toward this out of guilt, shame, or fear. People who give genuinely find joy in expressing love. Allowing the other person to experience this joy is intimate. In this exercise, you will practice genuine receptivity.

1. Create a practice of allowing yourself to receive. Here's a list of things you can practice gracefully receiving. Please highlight or circle any you're willing to practice.

    - Simply say "Thank you" when you receive a compliment, without returning it or deflecting it.
    - Accept someone's offer to do something for you, such as buy you lunch or clean up the house, by saying "Thank you" simply (please don't over-thank them or feel you must return the favor—you have the right to experience generosity).
    - Do something nice for yourself, like wear an outfit you've saved for a "nice" occasion or use that good lotion—being alive is the nice occasion!
    - Take "me" time to do something you want, like watch a movie you love or create art—do it even if you feel guilty.
    - Take yourself on a self-love date, such as to dinner and a movie.

    Please come up with as many ideas of receiving as you can—have fun with it:

    ____

    ____

    ____

    ____

    ____

    ____

    ____

2. You may feel uncomfortable during this practice, and please know that's okay. Sometimes when you are healing, it's uncomfortable, yet these "growing pains" guide you to recovery. You can tolerate this discomfort for the relief and happiness on the other side of it. You may want to affirm yourself, saying, "I deserve to receive and enjoy good things simply because I'm alive!"

Cultivating Healthy Relationship Skills Chapter Reminders

Congratulations! You've done powerful work in this chapter to cultivate the skills to act in a securely attached way with another person. To support you when you engage with others, please remember:

- Your self-relationship, which includes self-soothing your emotions and self-compassion, is the foundation of your relationship with others.
- You can act as if you are securely attached by remembering not to go to extremes in your behaviors due to nonsecure urges.
- Balancing how you communicate with another person involves both being respectful to them *and* respecting yourself.
- Setting boundaries is essential for a healthy, intimate relationship.
- Anger is a gift that reveals your needs and limits—you can honor your anger by setting boundaries *and* coping appropriately.
- Conflict is inevitable in any relationship; therefore, it's essential to cope well with intense emotions.
- Fear is natural in a relationship, and you can cope well with vulnerability.
- Letting yourself genuinely receive builds self-love *and* intimacy.

Chapter 9

THE ONGOING PRACTICE OF SECURE ATTACHMENT

Throughout this workbook, you've shown up for yourself in profoundly powerful ways. Learning to be your own securely attached caretaker allows you to transform your relationships from the inside out. Truly, there's nothing more important than attending to your relationship patterns. Over eight decades of research shows the single greatest predictor of a long, healthy life is having close relationships. Researchers discovered the happiest people in their relationships at age fifty were physically the healthiest at age eighty (Mineo 2017). Your future healthy, happy self is thanking you.

To best support your ongoing recovery, this chapter pulls together all the work you've done. Here, you'll develop strategies to simplify the ongoing practice of secure attachment. With time, your nonsecure thoughts and urges fade away until eventually, with continued practice, they feel like they happened a lifetime ago.

Your Nonsecure Parts Will Still Be Triggered

Moving forward, your nonsecure parts will still get triggered into anxious or avoidant thoughts and urges. This is human and not a failure. Recovery is simply about acting in healthier ways despite old, familiar urges. This is why mindfulness is so important. You can see the urge, pause, and act like your secure self. For instance, on my second date with my now-husband, my avoidant part was triggered. The combination of his kindness and attentiveness in addition to my genuine interest in him felt profoundly overwhelming. My impulse was to run for the hills as my fight-or-flight response was triggered. And yet, I breathed through it, realizing how hopeful and excited I was for this connection. Instead of running, I literally leaned into an embrace in that moment. Coping well with fear literally changed the trajectory of my whole life!

Moving forward, it's important to accept that your nonsecure parts will arise at times, while not giving them more power than they really have. They are only thoughts and feelings that you may validate and soothe.

EXERCISE: Relapse Prevention Planning

A primary way to protect your recovery is with a relapse prevention plan. This involves identifying the warning signs that you are reverting to anxious or avoidant thoughts or actions. Triggers are acknowledged as well. Mindful awareness of these signs and triggers enables you to plan ahead to protect your recovery. Reverting back to old familiar patterns is part of the recovery process sometimes. However, maintaining your recovery depends on your awareness so that you are able to intervene as a healthy parent as soon as possible. Now you'll identify your warning signs of relapse and coping strategies to protect your recovery.

Step One: You have cultivated a lot of awareness of your personal patterns. Remember, there is no shame in these behaviors and they're understandable. At the same time, you are completely capable of moving in a new direction. What are signs that you are acting or thinking in nonsecurely attached ways? Circle any warning signs here:

- Judging my desire to spend time with someone as negative
- Pushing someone away
- Suppressing and/or doubting my feelings, needs (including my nonnegotiable needs), wants, and boundaries
- Cheating
- Trying to fix another person
- Thinking someone will "save" me
- Feeling insecure and not "good enough"
- Brushing things under the rug
- Rushing a sexual relationship
- Lying
- Thinking if I can get my partner to change or understand me then I'll be okay
- Expecting someone to automatically forgive me and move on when I hurt them
- Using another person for attention, sex, money, or any other reason
- Creating emotional distance, such as by withholding vulnerability
- Pretending to be someone I'm not
- Creating physical distance, such as by being "too busy"
- Giving inauthentically, such as out of a sense of obligation or because I want to make myself irreplaceable
- Fantasizing that with the "right" person, I would never have misunderstandings
- Ignoring red flags
- Testing other people's commitment

- Asking for lots of reassurance and/or compliments
- Feeling resentment
- Believing I'm "better than" others
- Thinking my way is the "right" way
- Betraying myself, such as going back on my own boundaries
- Having a critical inner dialogue about myself and/or others
- Avoiding important conversations
- Refusing to advance a relationship with someone I care about, such as by refusing to label it
- Expecting perfection
- Fantasizing about escaping a relationship when there's conflict
- Being overly independent
- Not letting myself receive
- Getting stuck in fantasy thoughts that someone will change despite reality
- Spending all my time being with someone and/or obsessing about them
- Thinking I'll "die" if a relationship doesn't work out
- Ghosting someone
- Being unwilling to compromise whenever possible
- Feeling suffocated by someone
- Expecting others to read my mind
- Personalizing others' behavior
- Taking all the blame when there's conflict
- Valuing money, work, or anything else significantly more than my relationships
- Feeling used or like a doormat

- Thinking the other person is completely to blame when there's conflict
- Isolating
- Getting stuck in all-or-nothing thinking
- Becoming agitated or unkind when someone wants my attention or support
- Resenting when someone brings up their concerns

Step Two: Great job! There is no shame in how many warning signs you may have identified. Instead, we are celebrating your mindfulness! Look at the central theme of your warning signs. What is the simplest way you could describe this theme for yourself? Based on this description, what's one word you can keep in the back of your mind to stay mindful of this theme? Maybe, for instance, your core theme is doubting and betraying yourself. You could then focus on "self-trust" as an anchor word to interrupt this pattern and stay in recovery. Or if your theme is being inflexible with others, then you could use the word "openness" to help you stay grounded in recovery as another example. Write your anchor word here: ________

Step Three: Based on this central theme, create a personalized plan to support your ongoing recovery. The Resources in the back of the book can help you moving forward with this plan. Identify one thing you'd like to keep working on and create your plan. You want your future plan to honor this need while not overwhelming yourself. To help with this, you may pick three future action steps. If you doubt yourself, an example of your ongoing recovery plan could be:

1. Repeat the affirmation "I trust myself" at least once daily in the mirror.
2. Read a book on boundary-setting like *Setting Boundaries: 100 Ways to Protect Yourself, Strengthen Your Relationships, and Build the Life You Want...Starting Now!* (Mazzola Wood 2023)
3. Practice one skill from a book I choose at least once weekly.

Or if you tend to struggle with empathy for others, your plan might look like this:

1. Each day, ask myself, "What is one kind thing I can do for someone else without any strings attached?" (For example, buy someone in line a coffee or give an authentic compliment.)
2. Follow through on the answer to this question as simply as possible without making mental excuses.
3. Read a book like *Kindfulness*.

What are your next three action steps based on your central theme?

1. ______________________________

____

2. ______________________________

____

3. ______________________________

____

Step Four: By committing to this plan, you're guiding your whole Self in a harmoniously, securely attached way, which is an ongoing practice. When a warning sign arises, you'll benefit from comforting yourself as a securely attached parent. When a natural, human warning sign happens in the future, how can you comfort yourself? Consider self-soothing strategies you've cultivated, like deep breathing, taking a walk, or journaling.

____

____

____

____

Step Five: When a warning sign arises, it's important to be self-compassionate. You can do this with affirmations and self-soothing. At the same time, you will need to set limits on yourself to act in a secure way despite nonsecure urges. What limits may you need to set on yourself? For instance, if you become obsessive about someone, you could turn off your phone to stop checking it constantly. Or if you sometimes get stuck in thinking you're always right, you could meditate on loving-kindness or humility. Make it easier for yourself in the future by listing different strategies now:

____

____

____

____

Staying Present to Avoid Relapse

One of the biggest warning signs of relapse is becoming emotionally numb. This may happen because of numbing behaviors such as drinking, using drugs, overeating, or too much time online. Neglecting your self-care is another way you may become numb by getting too worn down. Or you may become numb if your past trauma is triggered and you move into a state of dissociation or depersonalization (not feeling present or real), which is the "frozen" state of fight-flight-freeze.

While understandable, numbing makes it more likely for you to relapse. If you're numb, you may feel like you no longer care about your recovery. This "eff it" attitude commonly precedes relapse. For example, if you get drunk, you may not care in the moment about texting your toxic ex for some "fun." Or if you're working too much, you may feel it's justified to use someone to blow off some steam. When you allow yourself to become, and stay, numb, you lose touch with your necessary balanced empathy for secure attachment. If you become numb to your own empathy, you are more likely to let others violate you. And you are more likely to harm others if you are numb to the painful impact you may have on them.

Finally, if you're numb or frozen, you may isolate more, which both anxiously and avoidantly attached people do at times. Polyvagal theory expert Deb Dana explains this as taking "refuge in disconnection" (2018). It doesn't need to be literal, either. The nonsecure parts of us sometimes feel like they have to disappear, for example by using substances to tolerate emotional or sexual intimacy. If this happens with someone, it's helpful to assess the threat. For instance, if you feel you have to get drunk to be with someone, this is a warning sign that you may feel unsafe with them. Otherwise, if this is a safe person for you, it's important to practice being more present to intimacy. You do this by protecting yourself against numbing behaviors to literally stay present.

EXERCISE: Staying Present to Whole Reality

You can interrupt this human tendency of reverting to old behaviors due to numbness by staying committed to a daily mindfulness practice. This may be as simple as the following exercise:

1. Ask yourself, "How present and whole do I feel right now?" You can use a scale like 0–10, or use words or a percentage out of 100. Most people automatically "know" the answer if they listen to their gut rather than their thinking mind. Listening to your intuition is an important part of recovery, as it helps keep you safe.

2. Most people aren't completely present when they initially check in. In addition to the noisiness of modern life, the wounds underlying nonsecure attachment may lead to a sense of being numb or not fully in your body. That's okay; just move on to the next step.

3. Can you invite more presence and wholeness back into your mind and body? Take deep breaths as you become more present, aware of your surroundings, and grounded. Use

whatever visualizations or activities feel right. For example, feel your body being supported by your seat or notice the items around you in detail.

4. If you're uncomfortable doing this, comfort yourself with affirmations such as "I'm safe being here" or "I can tolerate being more present even though it's uncomfortable." If you find an "edge" where you can no longer tolerate being more present, please stop for now. You're building your capacity to be more whole and present, which may take time. Depending on your wounds, this may be easier, or more difficult. That's okay. Please provide compassion for the part of you that feels safer being numb.

5. Commit to asking this question at least once a day to support your recovery. In the online tools for this workbook (available at http://www.newharbinger.com/55992), you will find a daily journaling worksheet with a variety of prompts, including this one.

The Fundamental Question for Secure Attachment

In addition to staying mindful of the signs of regression, it's important to stay focused on the qualities of secure attachment. This allows you to stay grounded into what recovery looks and feels like consistently. Moving forward, there is one essential question to keep coming back to for secure attachment: "Am I safe?" This necessitates there is no abuse present in the relationship. Of course, even healthy partners make mistakes and may disappoint or offend you at times. But healthy partners are committed to repairing the situation with you. This includes their taking genuine accountability for how they may have harmed you. True accountability means they take whatever action steps necessary to avoid harming you again. In a healthy relationship, your partner is your shelter in the storm, not the cause of your suffering in life.

If someone is unsafe for you, it's important to accept reality. To do this, interrupt excusing or justifying someone's mistreatment, as well as personalizing it. Someone being unsafe for you *is not and never will be a reflection of your worth.* It is simply a sign of their character. To answer the question of safety, it's important to explore the following as well:

- Are my nonnegotiable needs met? These needs are in addition to safety—and respect—which cannot be compromised. Nonnegotiable needs may include your values or life dreams, such as having children.

- Are they trustworthy and reliable? Trust means knowing they have your best interest in mind. Reliability means they are consistent. They say what they mean and mean what they say.

- Am I safe to them? This includes avoiding any abusive behaviors, no matter how upset you feel, by self-soothing. This also includes actively staying vulnerable and communicating your needs, concerns, and limits.

Letting Go to Move Forward

Moving forward into a new, securely attached future requires letting go of the past. This includes releasing attachments to past partners as well as your own toxic relationship patterns. This also involves fully accepting your wounds and no longer bargaining with this reality, such as wishing your childhood had been different. Accepting your past wounds allows you to fully move forward. It honors that your future is no longer defined by the past. Here, you no longer need to feel terrified of ever getting back into a toxic relationship. This is because by accepting the past, you fully integrate the lessons you've learned and can graduate to a new, healthier life.

By this point, you've probably realized there are certain behaviors or people you need to release. Setting boundaries on the things that harm you is an important responsibility, part of being a healthy inner parent. To do this, though, you must allow yourself to grieve and feel the full range of emotions attached to this loss. It is true you can both feel love and gratitude for someone (or a behavior) *and* need to let it go. To fully accept your past wounds, you must grieve the valid truth that you always deserved kindness, love, and respect, even though there were times you didn't receive this.

EXERCISE: Coping Well with Understandable Grief

Grief is a complex emotion that may take a long time to make peace with or process. The pain of some losses eventually fades away, like a breakup perhaps. The pain of other losses—such as seeing the truth that your father, for instance, has never been healthy for you and likely never will be—may never fully go away. Grief is best compared to waves in the ocean. Some days the sea is calm, and on other days, the waves are rocky and intense. On calm days, allow yourself to feel the peace. And when there's a rocky, grief-stricken day, validate yourself as a healthy parent, feel it, and soothe it.

In this activity, many coping skills for grief are provided to help as needed. If any strategies don't resonate with you, no problem—focus on the ones that sound personally useful or interesting. In the future when you feel grief, cope by using one of these strategies. You'll complete this activity by trying one strategy now.

Highlight the grief coping strategies that resonate with you as potentially helpful:

- Cry whenever needed (if you get lost in tears, though, set a timer for 10 to 20 minutes).
- Journal a goodbye letter to the toxic person—write anything and everything you'd want to say to them, knowing this is for your eyes only.
- Get rid of items that make you feel stuck or tied to the past (this includes digital items and social media connections).
- Make a collage representing your past, present, and future related to your trauma and recovery.
- Write a story about how you finally gained closure with your ex to use your fantasy thinking for your benefit.
- Get a Reiki session or watch one on YouTube related to cutting cords of grief.
- Pray to God, the Universe, or your higher self to surrender your pain and find peace.
- Go into nature, noticing how everything has its season.
- Do yoga, such as a Yin yoga class or one on the intestines or the lungs, which are connected to letting go and grief in Chinese Medicine (there are free classes on YouTube).
- Notice new stories to shift old ways of thinking; for example, to shift thinking that you can't trust women, journal about all the times a woman was reliable or nurturing.
- Visualize shedding your old skin and becoming your new secure Self.
- Listen to binaural beats to release the past.
- Take a bath and imagine the water collecting residue from your past, then watch it go down the drain.
- Journal a goodbye letter to one of your patterns that feels toxic—validate why it came into your life, then say goodbye.
- Do a guided meditation on grief.
- Attend EMDR (Eye Movement Desensitization and Reprocessing) therapy to help you make peace with the past.
- Create a release ritual, such as getting rid of all the items attached to someone you accept is toxic for you or writing a goodbye letter, and then burning the letter in a safe place.

Letting Go Through Forgiveness

Allowing yourself to cry, connecting to your spirituality, and being in nature are good coping strategies for grief. Another important grief coping strategy is practicing forgiveness. Like mindfulness, forgiveness is a practice. Often, it happens in stages, with the first step being the willingness to forgive. Once you're willing, you practice forgiving in different ways, such as meditating, praying, or journaling about it. See the Resources section in the back of this book to help with this process. Over time, you'll feel an eventual shift from an attachment to the past pain toward the relief of forgiveness. You practice forgiveness even when your hurts and anger are righteous and valid, to liberate you from the past.

More important than being willing to forgive others is the willingness to forgive yourself. A part of you may think you protect yourself from relapse if you judge yourself harshly for the past. However, judging yourself for your past choices chains you to old ways of being rather than freeing you. Forgiving yourself is different than feeling "sorry" for your past self. The latter reinforces the idea that you are powerless, which couldn't be further from the truth. You are tremendously powerful! Look at everything you did in this workbook. Forgiving yourself is an act of radical self-love; it honors your past suffering and acknowledges you're empowered to choose differently now. To help with this process, there's a free online tool you may use repeatedly to practice self-forgiveness, available at http://www.newharbinger.com/55992.

EXERCISE: Celebrating Yourself

To get to this point, you've done incredible healing work and have proven your courage time and again. The commitment you've shown indicates you are well prepared to act from your whole Self, who acts as a securely attached parent to all your parts. It's natural, though, if you second-guess your progress sometimes. Change tends to happen really slowly, and then all at once, you look around and your whole life is different! For this activity, please complete the following prompts.

1. Go back to the pie chart in chapter 1 where you outlined your current life and your hopes for the future.

2. In the pie chart below, note every way you've made progress from your previous self. Even if the changes are small or not yet consistent, this is a win. It's vital for your continued recovery that you take time to acknowledge your wins. This means celebrating not just the big wins, but the little ones too—like a loving parent!

MY LIFE NOW

How I feel when I wake up:
How I feel throughout the day:
My work is:
How I feel about myself:
How I feel about my ex (or partner) or the relationship:
My romantic/social life is:
How I care for my body:
How I care for my mental health:

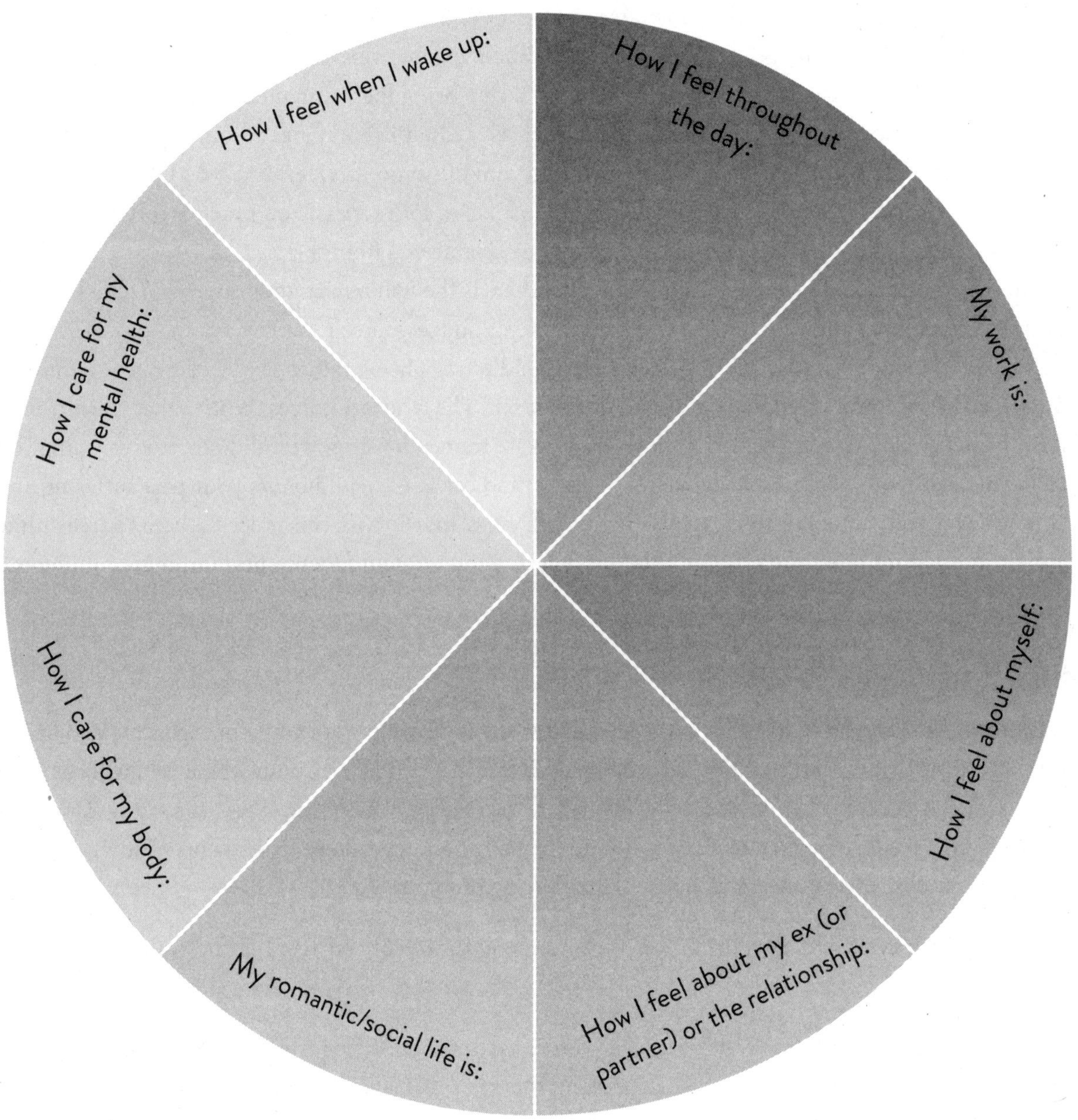

3. In the first chapter, you identified the first time you knew something was wrong in your relationship. Reflect on this situation again (you may need to review what you wrote, since sometimes we forget as we heal). How would you respond now if you found yourself in the same situation?

4. Write a love letter to yourself honoring how much work you've invested in recovering. Validate how challenging this process may have been or the times you felt like giving up. If you feel you made mistakes at times, validate this as a natural part of the change process. Making mistakes is often how we learn as human beings. Express your gratitude and love for yourself. Honor what lessons you are carrying with you from this point on.

5. What is today's date? ________________ This is now your official toxic relationship recovery date! You may make mistakes at times, but to maintain your recovery, you simply get back on track with your relapse prevention plan. Know you can never return to your initial place of suffering. As philosopher Heraclitus stated, "No man ever steps in the same river twice, for it's not the same river and he's not the same man."

6. Today (or this week), do something special for yourself. It can be *anything that feels meaningful for you*, such as going to a movie, buying yourself something you've been wanting (and can afford), or taking the afternoon off from work. Truly celebrate how far you've come.

7. Set a reminder in your phone for a year from now on today's date, to celebrate your anniversary!

EXERCISE: Moving Forward Joyfully

The path of healing is often bittersweet. You've likely experienced the bitter many times throughout this workbook. Now it's time to invite more sweetness into your life. This is the entire point of healing, after all! We get to a point where we have moved from chaos to stability. Rather than focusing on survival, you can spend your energy focused on thriving and experiencing more joy!

1. Remember how various wounds cause us to exile different parts of us? These exiles that get cut off are often your most alive, creative, and passionate parts. What is one creative and/or thrilling thing you've always wanted to do but felt too afraid, for whatever reason? This may be write a novel, go skydiving, learn to belly dance, or take a solo trip as examples.

   ____

   ____

   ____

2. If you never got to do this project or experience in your lifetime, how would you feel?

   ____

   ____

3. Can you reclaim your aliveness by working toward this goal? You may find yourself making excuses that there's "no time" right now. In reality, though, there will never be a "convenient" time to reclaim your exiles because these are the parts you're afraid of bringing back into

your life. What would it be like to invest even twenty minutes a week on this project, or to save even five dollars at a time for this activity? If you would feel regret if you never did this, what happens to this sense of regret when you allow yourself to reclaim your passions (even in baby steps)?

4. Is there anyone with whom you can share your goal of working toward what lights you up? (Feel free to message me too on social media—I'd love to know!)

5. Continue to practice reclaiming your joy—and for extra support, check out the activity "Reclaiming Authentic Joy" in your online tools at http://www.newharbinger.com/55992.

Congratulations!

The Ongoing Practice of Secure Attachment
Chapter Reminders

Throughout this process, you have been cultivating a secure attachment from within, centered from a place of wholeness. This lovely work has laid the foundation for your healthy, securely attached relationship in the future. In such a relationship, you honor that you are your partner's attachment figure by loving courageously and responsibly.

To get to this point, I'm in tremendous awe of you. Sadly, many people will never show themselves the love and commitment you've shown yourself here. At this point, you may not feel fully secure. Remember, that's okay. Secure attachment is a *practice* because you can never master emotional intimacy and vulnerability as a human being. You will naturally have scared thoughts and urges in the future. Staying securely attached is simply defined by your consistent willingness to soothe these scared parts and act from a centered, balanced place. Here, your life unfolds into more intimacy, joy, and connection as you accept there's no final destination to arrive at. To support your recovery, please remember:

- Staying mindful of your relapse warning signs and interrupting them as soon as you see them in a loving way is how you maintain—and grow—your recovery.
- Staying present to being grounded in your wholeness is essential to maintain your recovery.
- The most important question for a healthy relationship is "Am I safe?" (safe with and for them).
- Use the daily journal worksheet provided in the free online tools at http://www.newharbinger.com/55992 to stay on track.
- Keep practicing letting go and forgiving the past.
- Celebrate your wins.
- Remember to keep reclaiming joy; this is the whole point of recovering: to be happy and really live!

ACKNOWLEDGMENTS

To Ryan—Thank you for believing in the vision of this workbook and helping me find its voice. This project has been profoundly meaningful for me both professionally and personally. Thank you for making this workbook a reality—and many other books—to help countless people heal.

To Madeline—Thank you for cultivating a safe place for my creative process, understanding my intentions, and warmly helping me refine my message. Your insights shaped this workbook to be a much more helpful tool than it could've ever been without you.

To Amy—Since childhood, you have shown me more love, safety, and consistency than I ever experienced growing up in my family. You've shown me what it means to give and receive love from a place of cherishing the authentic being of the other person. Never once did you express judgment for the years I spent in relationships that harmed me, only showing empathy and trust that I'd find my way—and I'm so glad to now share life with you from this healed place. Thank you for always believing in me and encouraging me. I'm stronger because of you!

To Skitters and Ike—Thank you for being such joyful constant companions, including during writing time and yoga time. Thank you for reminding me there is always time to play ball! You add so much joy to our family!

To my Princess Kitty—You were my loyal companion and my cat best friend throughout the years I clung to toxic relationships most fiercely and genuinely questioned my worth. But when I saw myself in your eyes, I knew there was something lovable and worth protecting within me. It was my greatest dream I'd be able to find you a loving, safe, reliable cat-daddy in your lifetime as I recovered. Sadly, it didn't happen on the earthly realm, but I genuinely believe you see where I am now and are smiling. I carry you within me always.

To Cher—What a surprising, welcome gift our deepening relationship is for me! With my experiences in my family and rocky past, I never anticipated to feel so seen and celebrated by my mother-in-law. Thank you for your warm, loving acceptance and encouragement—it means more than you may know.

To Ethan—This project has involved personal excavation of my past before you. Thank you for holding the ever-loving, consistent, safe space to fully release wounds from the rocky path that guided me to you without judgment or misinterpretation. I have never met a person so firmly rooted in themselves as you. Your integrity and inner strength provide me endlessly safe, fertile ground for my expansion. With you, I feel I can soar because I have a safe place to land if I falter—and a safe place to celebrate when I am successful! There are no words for the way you help make my greatest life's dreams come true—including the "adventure of a lifetime," our long, happy marriage filled with safety, love, laughter, friendship, and understanding.

To my clients, past and present—Witnessing you wake up to the authentic beauty that has always been your innate self and reclaiming your birthright to safety, joy, and connection is a profound, humbling, and inspiring gift in my life. There are no words for my appreciation that you placed your vulnerable trust in me to be an ally in your healing. This workbook could not exist without you. Thank you.

To you, dear reader—The people who have the fortune of never experiencing toxic relationship patterns may never fully understand just how much courage it takes to sometimes fight tooth and nail to recover. But I see you and your internal strength. I'm in awe of you and I'm rooting you on with every word you read.

RESOURCES

If You Want to Find a Therapist

Psychology Today Directory—https://www.psychologytoday.com/us/therapists

If you want trauma-specific therapy, you may filter the search for therapists who offer EMDR (Eye Movement Desensitization and Reprocessing), which is a highly effective therapy treatment model, or Brainspotting, which research is showing as another effective trauma therapy.

If You Need Extra Support Because You Are in an Abusive Relationship

Please be mindful that searches and websites may be discovered by your partner on a shared computer or if they know your passwords. If needed, access any sites you don't want your partner knowing you visited from a computer in a space where your partner doesn't have access (such as at work or the public library) and while not logged into any accounts, i.e., don't log into your Google accounts.

National Domestic Violence Hotline
https://www.thehotline.org/
Provides tools for safety planning and local resources to support you

Further Reading for Trauma Healing

The Body Keeps the Score: Brain, Mind, and Body in the Healing of Trauma by Bessel van der Kolk

Healing Sexual Trauma Workbook: Somatic Skills to Help You Feel Safe in Your Body, Create Boundaries, and Live with Resilience by Erika Shershun

The Nervous System Workbook: Practical Exercises to Ease Anxiety, Find Safety, and Come Home to Yourself Using Polyvagal Theory by Deb Dana

Therapeutic Yoga for Trauma Recovery: Applying the Principles of Polyvagal Theory for Self-Discovery, Embodied Healing, and Meaningful Change by Arielle Schwartz

Further Reading to Love Your Authentic Self as a Healthy Parent

Confidently Authentic: A Self-Love Blog (www.confidentlyauthentic.com)

The Inner Child Workbook: What to Do with Your Past When It Just Won't Go Away by Cathryn L. Taylor

Self-Compassion: The Proven Power of Being Kind to Yourself by Kristin Neff

The Self-Forgiveness Workbook: Mindfulness and Compassion Skills to Overcome Self-Blame and Find True Self-Acceptance by Grant Dewar

Further Reading for Healthy Relationship Skills

Attached: The New Science of Adult Attachment and How It Can Help You Find—and Keep—Love by Amir Levine and Rachel S. F. Heller

The Science of Trust: Emotional Attunement for Couples by John M. Gottman

Setting Boundaries: 100 Ways to Protect Yourself, Strengthen Your Relationships, and Build the Life You Want ...Starting Now! by Krystal Mazzola Wood

You Are the One You've Been Waiting For: Applying Internal Family Systems to Intimate Relationships by Richard C. Schwartz

Further Reading for Mindfulness

Kindfulness by Ajahn Brahm

A New Earth: Awakening to Your Life's Purpose by Eckhart Tolle

The Power of Now: A Guide to Spiritual Enlightenment by Eckhart Tolle

The Untethered Soul: The Journey Beyond Yourself by Michael Singer

YouTube Resources for Further Recovery Support:

Black Yogi Nico Marie (mindful movement, inner peace, alignment, and self-love)
https://www.youtube.com/@YogaWithNico

Confidently Authentic | Krystal Mazzola Wood
https://www.youtube.com/@krystalmazzola_wood

Dr. Kristin Neff (self-compassion resources)
https://www.youtube.com/@NeffKristin/videos

Taylor's Tracks Yoga (Yin and vinyasa yoga, self-confidence)
https://www.youtube.com/@TaylorsTracks

REFERENCES

American Heart Association. 2024. "Elevated Stress Hormones Linked to Higher Risk of High Blood Pressure and Heart Events." *Hypertension Journal Report.* Accessed June 24, 2024.

Batanova, M., R. Weissbourd, and J. McIntyre. 2024. *Loneliness in America: Just the Tip of the Iceberg?* Making Caring Common, October.

Bretherton, I. 1992. "The Origins of Attachment Theory: John Bowlby and Mary Ainsworth." *Developmental Psychology* 28(5): 759–775.

Dana, D. 2018. *The Polyvagal Theory in Therapy: Engaging in the Rhythm of Regulation.* New York: W. W. Norton & Company.

David, S. 2017. "The Gift and Power of Emotional Courage." TED, TEDWomen 2017, posted January 30, 2018. 17:51.

Emery, L. F., W. L. Gardner, K. L. Carswell, and E. J. Finkel. 2018. "You Can't See the Real Me: Attachment Avoidance, Self-Verification, and Self-Concept Clarity." *Personality and Social Psychology Bulletin* 44(8): 1133–1146.

Gottman, J. 2011. *The Science of Trust: Emotional Attunement for Couples.* New York: W. W. Norton & Company.

Hill, N. 2023. *Wellness.* New York: Alfred A. Knopf.

Holt-Lunstad, J. 2021. "Is Social Disconnection Comparable to Smoking?" TED, TEDxBYU, posted May 4, 2021. 12:43.

Kjærvik, S. L., and B. J. Bushman. 2024. "A Meta-Analytic Review of Anger Management Activities That Increase or Decrease Arousal: What Fuels or Douses Rage?" *Clinical Psychology Review* 109: 102414.

Levine, A., and R. S. F. Heller. 2010. *Attached: The New Science of Adult Attachment and How It Can Help You Find—and Keep—Love.* New York: TarcherPerigee.

Levine, P., and A. Frederick. 1997. *Waking the Tiger: Healing Trauma.* Berkeley, CA: North Atlantic Books.

Mazzola, K. 2019. *The Codependency Recovery Plan: A 5-Step Guide to Understand, Accept, and Break Free from the Codependent Cycle*. Emeryville, CA: Althea Press.

Mazzola Wood, K. 2023. *Setting Boundaries: 100 Ways to Protect Yourself, Strengthen Your Relationships, and Build the Life You Want...Starting Now!* Stoughton, MA: Adams Media.

Mineo, L. 2017. "Good Genes Are Nice, but Joy Is Better." *Harvard Gazette*, April 11.

Neff, K. 2011. *Self-Compassion: The Proven Power of Being Kind to Yourself*. New York: William Morrow.

Saxena, M., S. Tote, and B. Sapkale. 2023. "Multiple Personality Disorder or Dissociative Identity Disorder: Etiology, Diagnosis, and Management." *Cureus* 15(11): e49057.

Schwartz, R. C. 2023. *You Are the One You've Been Waiting For: Apply Internal Family Systems to Intimate Relationships*. Boulder, CO: Sounds True.

Set, Z. 2019. "Potential Regulatory Elements Between Attachment Styles and Psychopathology: Rejection Sensitivity and Self-Esteem." *Noro Psikiyatri Arsivi* 56(3): 205–212.

Siegel, D., and T. Payne Bryson. 2012. *The Whole-Brain Child: 12 Revolutionary Strategies to Nurture Your Child's Developing Mind*. New York: Bantam.

Steil, R., A. Schneider, and L. Schwartzkopff. 2022. "How to Treat Childhood Sexual Abuse Related PTSD Accompanied by Risky Sexual Behavior: A Case Study on the Use of Dialectical Behavior Therapy for Posttraumatic Stress Disorder (DBT-PTSD)." *Journal of Child and Adolescent Trauma* 15: 471–478.

Yanguas, J., S. Pinazo-Henandis, and F. J. Tarazona-Santabalbina. 2018. "The Complexity of Loneliness." *Acta Biomedica: Atenei Parmensis* 89(2): 302–314.

Krystal Mazzola Wood, LMFT, is CEO of the Healthy Relationship Foundation, where she supports clients in recovering from trauma, codependency, and toxic relationships. Mazzola Wood is best-selling author of two books on codependency recovery: *The Codependency Recovery Plan* and *The Codependency Workbook*. She is also author of *Setting Boundaries* and *Confidently Authentic*, a self-love and personal growth blog for support in living intentionally and building healthy, fulfilling relationships. She lives in Phoenix, AZ, with her husband and their rescue pets: a cat and a dog.